CW00502688

ABOUT THE AUTHOR

Since 1992, Darren has demonstrated his mediumship publicly and privately around the UK and internationally. He conveys evidence from the 'other side' with astounding accuracy. He is also recognised as a motivational and inspiring teacher of mediumship and there is high demand for his public demonstrations and seminars.

You can find more information about Darren and his work at www.darrenbrittain.co.uk

FROM INNOCENCE TO INNER SENSE

THE JOURNEY TO MEDIUMSHIP

DARREN BRITTAIN

Copyright © 2020 Darren Brittain

The moral right of the author has been asserted.

Apart from any fair dealing for the purposes of research or private study, or criticism or review, as permitted under the Copyright, Designs and Patents Act 1988, this publication may only be reproduced, stored or transmitted, in any form or by any means, with the prior permission in writing of the publishers, or in the case of reprographic reproduction in accordance with the terms of licences issued by the Copyright Licensing Agency. Enquiries concerning reproduction outside those terms should be sent to the publishers.

Matador
9 Priory Business Park,
Wistow Road, Kibworth Beauchamp,
Leicestershire. LE8 0RX
Tel: 0116 279 2299
Email: books@troubador.co.uk
Web: www.troubador.co.uk/matador
Twitter: @matadorbooks

ISBN 978 1800460 829

British Library Cataloguing in Publication Data.
A catalogue record for this book is available from the British Library.

Printed and bound in the UK by TJ International, Padstow, Cornwall
Typeset in 11pt Ten Oldstyle by Troubador Publishing Ltd, Leicester, UK

Matador is an imprint of Troubador Publishing Ltd

MIX
Paper from responsible sources
FSC® C013056

CONTENTS

Foreword by Tricia Robertson ix
Introduction xi

1 Awakening 1
2 Awareness 9
3 Realisation 23
4 Reality 30
5 The Process 42
6 Experiential Mediumship 63
7 Evidence 72
8 Boundaries 82
9 Development 93
10 Mind 111
11 Power 120
12 Connection 128
13 Breathing 138
14 People 147
15 Environment 153
16 Language 159
17 Expression 164
18 Final Thoughts 171

FOREWORD BY TRICIA ROBERTSON

I have observed Darren demonstrate his mediumship many times through the years. He has always impressed me with his appearance, demeanour and in his manner of speaking to an intended recipient. The evidential content of his readings is invariably striking and his standards are high. He also delivers the information from a loved one with empathy and compassion which results in his work bringing great hope and comfort to many.

In this book he details his journey to become the medium that he is today in a clear and, at times, exciting manner. His journey, like many mediums, has not always been an easy one, but his intelligence and perseverance has seen him through the uncertain times.

This book is not brought forth from ego but an obvious desire to help budding mediums address the subject of mediumship and development in the best possible way. He also has a well-expressed, engaging, interesting and profound use of language on occasion.

Although I am not a medium, I really enjoyed this book and can see that it should help any medium who wishes to develop or improve their work. From his own experience, Darren lays out some of the pitfalls of becoming a medium and is now able to give you the benefit of his own mistakes by giving clear advice and direction in various aspects of your work.

The overall sense of this book is that it speaks the truth in a manner that is easy to follow.

Everyone with an interest in mediumship should read this book; it is one of the best that I have ever read. It is easily read, very informative and very enjoyable. No developing medium should miss this opportunity to gain from his experience.

Tricia J Robertson: author, lecturer, broadcaster, psychical researcher, past president of the Scottish Society for Psychical Research and founder member of PRISM.

Tricia's books: *Things You Can Do When You're Dead*, *More Things You Can Do When You're Dead* and, awaiting, *It's Life and Death, but Not as You Know It.*

INTRODUCTION

It was so hot you could smell the tar on the pavement as I waited to cross the road. My shoes were almost sticking to the ground as I walked with my brother, Kevin, to the bus stop. It was Saturday, our day to visit my grandparents who lived about four miles away in a small South Yorkshire town called Thorne. For as long as I could remember, we made that trip every Saturday.

Saturdays generated a certain amount of excitement, as my nanna would usually have baked cakes and there were always some kind of 'goodies' waiting for us there. However, this particular Saturday seemed somehow different. I didn't feel my usual excitement and I had an odd sensation in my head. The sensation was nagging, like a dull pressure, a heaviness but also as though my head was full of cotton wool. I tried not to think about it too much and attributed it to the late hour that I'd gone to bed the night before. Late nights only ever seem a good idea when you're not recovering from one, and at least I could catch up with my rest over the weekend, or so I thought.

I shifted my focus back to crossing the road to catch the bus, I was half way across when something happened that terrified me. I was trying my best to hold a conversation with Kevin when I suddenly became aware of a strange 'light' in front of me. It wasn't a very big light, but big enough to draw my attention. As much as I tried to follow it, the light moved away from me and obscured my vision in that area. I felt curious about what was happening; it was something I'd never experienced before. Kevin had noticed that I was acting oddly, and I'd started to feel weirdly disconnected from everything around me, like being in a strange, invisible bubble where life was happening and yet I wasn't involved.

I was beginning to feel scared; I started rubbing my eyes to try and shake the 'light' from my head. In the five minutes it took to wait for the bus, my vision had deteriorated so much that I became frightened of what might happen in the next few minutes. I was desperate to sit down, certain that if I didn't I'd collapse into a big heap on the floor at the bus stop. I was constantly asking Kevin if he could see the bus coming: "What time is it?", "Why is it taking so long?" I was chasing the light in my vision, trying to outrun it, trying to push it away and all the time monitoring whether the light was bigger than before. "Should I go home?", "Where is this bus?" Every thought I had swung between, "It'll be gone in a minute," to, "What if it doesn't?" Each thought was accompanied by the rising feeling of fear and nausea in my stomach.

After what felt like an eternity the bus finally arrived; the sign on the front usually said 'Moorends 250' but I could only see the M and the 0 – the other characters had vanished along with any sense of normality. I asked Kevin to get on first so I could place my hand on his back to guide me. At this point I didn't trust my vision at all; I looked down and all I could see was a blank space where the step should have been. As I stepped on, the reality of what I was experiencing hit me and it felt devastating, like an avalanche. I was fourteen years old and I might actually be losing my sight.

I didn't see the hand of the driver as he accepted my two-pence fare, nor could I focus on his voice; the only thing that mattered in that moment was taking place in my head. I looked around for some stability and in my peripheral vision I could see a part of a handrail; like a toddler finding his feet for the first time, I reached out to steady myself. I was frightened of falling down, so I again placed one hand on Kevin's back and the other hand was holding the cold comforting metal of the handrail beside me; my knuckles were sore from gripping it so tightly, but it offered me some reassurance. I shuffled slowly along the aisle of the bus, staying close to the side. All I wanted to do was to sit down, I didn't care where, whichever seat was closest. At least half of my vision had now gone and the blank spots had been replaced by shimmering, zig-zag forms. I would try to focus on them, hold them in my gaze so that I could see what they were and I might then understand what was happening, but no, each time I looked to see it, it moved. It appeared that the zig-zag forms were dancing in front of me, almost mocking me by escaping my vision. "I'm going to go blind and never see the faces of the people I love again." I started to panic, convincing myself I should get off the bus and somehow find a way back home where I would still be able to see my loved ones before the inevitable happened.

The fear was so overwhelming that I was starting to sweat and go clammy; it felt like I was drifting further and further away from reality. By this point I'd lost awareness of my brother; I'd became so absorbed by this experience I couldn't focus on him beside me – even his presence wasn't a comfort. Then it started, at the back of my head at first. Like being punched with full force, a pain so intense that I wanted to be sick. Slowly it moved to the right side, pulsating, throbbing and so acute that even my hair started to hurt – how was that possible? I followed the pain, monitoring it moment to moment to assess whether it was worse than a minute ago, trying in some way to work out what came next but not daring to think what that might even be. The pain continued to intensify and it was like nothing I'd ever felt before. It felt like a nail was being driven into my scalp, a pain so sharp and so severe that every beat of my heart could be felt through the pulse in my right temple. I dared not move, fearful that any activity would make it worse and would result in my vomiting and embarrassing myself in public.

Apparently at this point I was pale and sweating badly; my brother kept asking me if I was OK and he was counting down the bus stops to when we could get off. "Just breathe deeply," I kept thinking. My eyes had now become painful, as though they were being squeezed from inside, and the light coming through the window was piercing, so much so that I sat with my eyes closed, desperately trying to find relief. "Not long now, Daz," Kevin would say every so often, probably scared himself of what was happening and feeling powerless to help. I'd noticed that my senses had become incredibly heightened; every noise was amplified and the chatter of people on the bus became tortuous. The feeling of people passing my seat to get on or off was distressing – they would brush past me and the sensation of them against my leg was painful, even my skin hurt. I instinctively flinched away when I heard the bell ring or the bus coming to a stop.

This was the longest, and most painful, twenty-minute journey I'd ever taken. Every part of my body was struggling, not to mention my mind, which by this time was overwhelmed with thoughts of despair and fear. "Next stop and we're off, Daz, Nanna will know what to do."

Kevin rang the bell and I waited until the bus had completely stopped; the thought of getting up and walking on a moving bus in my current state was unimaginable. The feel of the fresh air on my skin as I stepped off the bus was almost cleansing, and whilst the warmth of the morning sun did nothing to ease the pain in my head, the knowledge that in a few minutes time I could lie down was enough to make me walk faster. We walked silently, but determinedly, both focussed on the pain in my head and also on reaching my Nannas house, the place I always loved to be. Finally, we arrived, to be met by the familiar smell of furniture polish that Nanna loved to use, and the earthy smell of the coal Grandad had used to lay the fire for that evening. The relief was immense. Nothing altered the pain in my head and I was still trying to breathe my way through it, but I felt safe. I took time to explain to Nanna what had happened, then I went upstairs, tucked myself in under layers of bedding, curled into a ball and, with a bucket by the side of the bed just in case, I fell into a deep sleep until late that afternoon.

CHAPTER 1

AWAKENING

I came out of the doctor's surgery not really understanding the nature of migraines. Mum used to have attacks, which completely disabled her and put her in bed for days at a time, so she knew that what I had experienced was very common. It took a while to absorb that there were several triggers I had to avoid to prevent the headaches returning. The most common triggers were cheese and chocolate. Chocolate I ate a lot of and cheese rarely. I found the thought of no more chocolate as painful as the headache itself! If eating cheese and chocolate were the only triggers it wouldn't have been that bad, but I soon found that activities such as running, or even sneezing, would bring about severe visual disturbances and pain, necessitating a lie down in a darkened room. Strong smells, bright lights and loud noises seemed to result in almost daily attacks which began to disable and disconnect me more and more from the outside world. When I wasn't unwell, I was recovering, and regardless of whether I had headaches or not, I was still seeing lights around everyone I looked at. Concerned by this, my mum felt we should get my eyes tested.

The optician was a tall, wiry man with steel-rimmed spectacles, the type you would see on mad scientists in old horror films. My mum explained the situation to him and he raised his eyebrows. I was told to read from a board with letters on it – stupid, I thought. I instinctively knew that there wasn't a problem with my eyesight. In fact, I didn't think there was a problem at all, but being fourteen and with my mum giving me the 'Don't you dare show me up!' look, I did as I was told.

It's strange what you observe when you're feeling vulnerable, isn't it? The room wasn't very clean and there were stains on the carpet which looked like trodden-in chewing gum. One of the legs on the table had a dent in it and there was a piece of sellotape stuck to the ceiling, probably from last year's Christmas decorations; it was not the most hygienic of places. The optician himself had a very large mole on his chin in the shape of a baked bean and, judging by the smell of his breath, was recovering from an indulgent night before. The equipment he used looked scuffed, dated somehow, and there was a stuffiness in the room. The room was well lit, so well lit you could see the flecks of dust passing through the sunshine shining through the window.

The optician closed the blinds and then shone lights into both of my eyes for what seemed like an hour, before finally exclaiming that there was nothing wrong with my eyes at all. The optometrist asked me to explain again exactly what I saw.

I took a deep breath and started to speak. "The light around you is blue," I said, pointing to his left side. "It's about an inch thick, and I only see it around your arm, but I have a feeling that it's everywhere. It's a vibrant blue, almost shining, and it's weird that it kind of vibrates." I couldn't think of how else to describe it, and the more I described it, the more furrowed his brow became.

"And you see this all the time?" he asked.

"I see it mainly when I'm in mathematics," I explained. "It's usually when I'm daydreaming, or if I really try to look for it."

Whilst it wasn't unusual for migraine sufferers to experience visual disturbances during an attack, he wasn't able to explain what I was seeing when I wasn't experiencing one and he had no explanation for the light I saw around him that day. It was 'possibly ocular migraine', but nothing definitive, he said.

Ocular migraines are defined as temporary visual disturbances that can affect one or both eyes and are similar to the visual disturbances of the migraine headache, but minus the headache. The visual symptoms are thought to be caused by a reduced blood flow to the brain, in the same way as a migraine with a headache and they generally only last for twenty to thirty minutes. This definition did not fit the way I was occasionally able to tune in to, or away from, seeing the lights, or how they would sometimes remain for longer than thirty minutes. It also occurred to me that when I was having a full migraine attack, I would seemingly lose parts of my vision, there would be blank spots, or scotoma, as it's called.

When I was looking at the lights, yet not experiencing any headache, I didn't get those same blank areas; if anything, I was seeing more. There was no change to what I experienced with my physical senses – I was still able to see the person clearly, I could interact with them, hear and chat with them as normal, and there was no change in my behaviour either, I was just able to see the lights as well.

For three years the doctors had tried various types of medication, without success, and not only did the headaches continue during that period, I'd also lost so much time from school that I was getting behind in my school work. A couple of the teachers even started to make remarks such as, "Nice of you to show up," or, "You'll never amount to anything if you don't come to school." Of course, this did not contribute positively to my self-esteem, which in turn caused me more stress, and more stress led to more headaches.

Finally, after multiple trips to my GP, receiving a different prescription at almost every visit, we came across a medication that seemed to do the trick. It was a preventative treatment called Pizotifen, and rather than taking pills once the headache had started (which had little effect), I would take these daily before I went to bed. Within days of taking Pizotifen the headaches stopped. I could run, cough, sneeze – in fact, do everything and anything – and the headaches did not manifest; it was like my life had been given back to me. It really felt miraculous! The one thing, however, that hadn't changed was the lights that I continued to see around people. As before, there were different shapes, and they moved, vibrated and shone in all manner of hues and colours. I just accepted it was 'ocular migraine', as the optician had suggested, and gave them no other significance; I was just so grateful that I didn't have the painful headaches anymore.

I wasn't the stereotypical teenager – loud, difficult or the 'up and down moody' sort that you hear about. I was the type who preferred his own company and whom few wanted to befriend; I always felt different somehow. I didn't really have many friends at school – apart from Martin, who shared the same sense of humour – but otherwise, I was socially awkward and I never felt comfortable talking to anyone. My bedroom was my 'safe place' and I'd rarely leave it unless it was to go to school, visit my friend Martin or to take the weekend trip to my grandparents. I remember saving my pocket money weekly so I could buy my very own portable TV for my room, and when I finally got my grey JVC fourteen-inch colour TV, I went out even less. I would normally dress in only dark colours as I didn't want to stand out, and I certainly wasn't comfortable with any attention. Looking back, I was a lonely child, and most of the time I felt something was wrong with me. I knew I was probably gay but felt ashamed of it, and by the very nature of shame, the easiest way of concealing it was to hide myself away, hence being so difficult to reach. I'm sure my parents were secretly worried. By comparison, my brother was the opposite – outgoing and lively – and he took every opportunity to be outside.

While I was polite to people, I avoided eye contact with those I didn't know and would go out of my way to avoid anyone who might speak to me. By this time, I'd accepted the 'lights', and learned to not speak about them; after all, if no-one else saw them, it was yet more of a reason for people to think I was 'weird', an opinion I felt sure they already held.

Nothing changed for a while; I was able to go to school regularly and had decided that, rather than stay on to do my A levels, I would leave after my GCSEs and take an electrician's apprenticeship. My dad is a joiner, and all the men in the family came from a working-class skilled background so it felt right to do the same. Not being particularly physically strong, applying to become a bricklayer or a builder was not what I felt drawn to, but I liked the idea of the skill involved in electrical work, so I signed up. An apprenticeship would mean that four days a week I would have an employer who would provide 'on the job' training. On a Monday, from morning to afternoon, I would attend Doncaster College to learn the theory of the subject. The first course was 'City & Guilds 236 – Electrical Installation Competences'. My life at that point seemed pretty mapped out. I intended to be a fully qualified electrician and once I'd learned to drive, I'd be able to start my own business; all seemed well. The first part of this 'plan' progressed as expected: I left school, signed up to the scheme, and began to work installing warden call systems and alarms for a local company. It was then that something interrupted the plan.

I can't say there was a bang or a flash of light, nor was there a choir of angels or a disembodied voice calling my name. I saw no spirits, felt no presences, nor did I have objects flying around the room pointing me towards the paranormal or pulling me towards an unseen world. I just woke up one morning after a particularly good night's sleep with the most insatiable desire to explore the supernatural.

It was a feeling I'd never experienced before, and I didn't understand where it came from or why it was there. None of that mattered; the important thing was that I listened to it and followed the feeling urging me to explore it. At that stage I only looked at it as it being an interest – never in my life had I even thought of the paranormal, let alone wanted to delve into its hidden treasures, and without any previous experiences of the paranormal, I had nothing to fear either. Some mediums will tell you that they always saw things as a child or how they would play with spirit children – not me. Until that morning, I knew nothing of the Spirit World and I had no idea what to do or where to go for guidance and to find out more. It happened to be a Monday morning and the college I attended was opposite the town's main library. It seemed as though the library would be the perfect place to start my search.

The parapsychology section was number 133, the same number of my house – an interesting coincidence, I thought. The atmosphere of the library lent itself to my enquiries; everyone was in their own world and it was deathly quiet. I'd never been in the library before, and what struck me most was that everything was green: the carpet tiles, the curtains, the vinyl chairs, and even the pictures contained plants, trees and green! Feeling uncomfortable about people thinking I was mad, I made my way to the relevant section and avoided making eye contact with anyone on my way. Section 133 was tucked away in the far corner of the room, which was perfect as that area offered me privacy. I wondered whether they'd designed the layout to keep the 'weird stuff' and the weird people out of view? I grabbed the first book I could find and sat down to read. I don't remember the title of it; there were so many books I'd scanned through within the hour of my lunch break. The word 'psychic' kept cropping up in many of the books. A psychic person, I understood, was 'someone who was able to see, hear and feel things that were beyond the reasoning of the five physical senses'. Reading that sentence made me feel a bit odd. I did see things that other people couldn't and I also knew things about people without being told. It was true! I'd already learned that if I stared enough at the lights for long enough they would somehow tell me things. I also knew that certain colours meant different things: grey was physical pain, red was anger, green was stress and yellow was joy. I could also tell by the way the light around a person moved whether they were depressed or anxious, and I could sometimes feel in my own body what they were experiencing too. The books confirmed my experiences, although their interpretation of the colours differed from book to book, as well as differing from my own view. All the books agreed that there was a name for these lights, a name which, strangely, happened to be the same one the doctor called them – the lights I was seeing were called an aura.

Now I had a name for what I was seeing and I didn't feel that I was the only person this was happening to. I had left the library that day with more questions than books, but I still needed to find out more; it was one thing to find out the name of the lights, but I still needed to know how I was seeing these lights and, more importantly, why. Was I one of these 'psychic' people and, if so, what was the purpose behind it? I reasoned that books couldn't give me all the answers I craved. I needed to find where these psychic people 'hung out' so I could learn more. I didn't have to wait too long for the answers.

CHAPTER 2

AWARENESS

A dark, run-down old building held most of the answers to the questions I had. It stood on the main road in the village next to mine, and people referred it as the 'spooky hut'. There were stories circulating in school about how people entered the spooky hut fit and well yet would come out possessed by a demon! Apparently, some attendees at the spooky hut had allegedly floated around inside the building and spoken in a Native American accent, claiming to be Chief Sitting Bull or some other well-known dead person. People easily frightened by these stories dared not even walk on the same side of the street as the building. Those who weren't scared enjoyed tormenting the younger kids with stories of what might happen if they found themselves in close proximity to the hut.

There were tales of people seeking out others who 'knew things' – in fact, could read the future – or who had some kind of spiritual 'gifts'. It was these reports that intrigued me the most. The spooky hut was in reality the Spiritualist Church; I used to pass it on the bus journey on the weekly visits to my grandparents. In fact, the bus stop was literally in front of the building, so I couldn't miss it. I had always wondered what actually went on in there, even though I had not the courage to ask anyone who might know. The only way for me to know was to pay it a visit and see for myself. Of course, that would mean risking attack by a demon, or an Indian chief, or being lifted off the floor by an invisible force, but so long as I would be helped to understand what was happening to me, that was just fine! On my next trip past the church, I paid attention to the service times and promised myself that I would visit.

On Wednesdays there was something called 'open circle'; I remembered reading somewhere that psychic people often sat in circles to help 'develop' their abilities while quietly waiting for spirits to contact them. I wasn't too keen on the idea of waiting for ghosts to appear, but I did want to understand what I was experiencing, and as scary as this place seemed, as well as the books, it presented another source of information.

The following Wednesday arrived, but unfortunately so had the fog. It had descended like a heavy blanket and it stubbornly showed no signs of moving on. As I walked along, people appeared like ghostly silhouettes, the fog stripping away their identity; there was nothing to define who they were until they got closer. The sight of them did nothing to alleviate the thoughts in my head about what I was to experience when I arrived at the church. The footprints of ghostly figures glistened with frost and there was a distinct smell of fear in the air. It was 18 December 1991 and the fear was my own.

The walk to the church was about ten minutes, but I decided to walk slowly so that I could pray. It's strange that when you're frightened you can actually remember all the words to the Lord's Prayer isn't it? Even though I'd had no occasion to say the prayer since I'd left primary school, I remembered it exactly. I had never been one for praying, but the thought of what might happen to me that night made me find my spiritual voice. As I walked, the hue of the streetlights cast an eerie glow into the fog; there was not a soul about, and the thoughts of floating ghosts and demons filled my head. "Our Father who art in Heaven..." I began. I started to feel a little calmer until I got to, "...and deliver us from all evil," when I suddenly reminded myself of what I was frightened of! I prayed harder. I prayed so hard that I felt as though I was gritting my teeth. "I'll sit near the doors," I thought, "and if anything floats, moves, or speaks Red Indian, I'm off!"

More than once I stopped and questioned whether I should – or indeed, could – go in. "What if they are crazy people; what if I'm in danger?" I'd convinced myself that I'd decide when I got there. I could always go another time if I changed my mind; in fact, the truth was, I didn't have to go in at all, ever. The service started at 7pm; I'd left home at 6.30pm and I was ten minutes early. When I arrived, there were a few people gathered at the front of the church, mostly women.

I suddenly felt very frightened and alone. I really wanted to go in, but I didn't want to go in on my own, and the fear of being possessed by a spirit, thrown around by one, or spoken to by anyone living or dead terrified me.

As I approached the gate, there was a grandmotherly lady, nicely dressed with curly grey hair and a warm smile. "Surely she couldn't be involved in anything spooky; she looks too normal," I thought. Without realising what I was doing, I desperately reached out and touched her arm. "Do you mind if I come in with you, please? I've never been before, and I don't know what you do in there, but I'm really interested!" I spoke the whole sentence without taking a breath.

"Of course you can, luv," she said, and so I followed her in.

True to my promise to myself, I sat very near the entrance. The room was quite large, square with twenty-four black leather chairs set out in a circle. The ceiling beams were painted black and the roof went up into an apex. I was quite surprised to see that there were already about nineteen people seated and they were chatting to each other quite happily, not solemnly and quietly as I had expected. The room was painted a very pale shade of blue and there was a stage at the far end of the church hosting an arrangement of flowers on a small table. On the wall above the flowers was painted the legend, 'GOD IS THE SPIRIT OF TRUTH' in broad gold lettering. "Reassuring that they have a god at least!" I thought. My eyes were very wide as I noticed every detail about my surroundings and the people I was with. The assembly was mainly women, of all ages, but the majority were over fifty. There was an air of excitement and a sense of 'fullness' in the room, something I hadn't expected to feel. The few churches I'd been in felt very different. I had experienced them as hollow and empty; this space certainly wasn't like that. The service was about to begin.

We were welcomed by the leader of the circle and she explained that we would start the evening with a hymn and a prayer. When I arrived there had been a hymn-book on the chair; I had already put it under my seat, as I had no intention of singing. I was already planning on being invisible and singing wouldn't help that! The hymn began:

Open my eyes that I may see,
Glimpses of truth Thou hast for me,
Help me to set the Higher Self free,
So, shall I serve and worship Thee.
Silently now, I wait for Thee
Ready my God, Thy will to see
Open my eyes, Illumine me
Spirit Divine

I listened intently to the lyrics, and they resonated such that I wanted to read them, so I picked up my hymn-book and found the relevant page. The lyrics were so apt, it was as if they spoke directly to me and my need for being there. After two more verses, it was time for the prayer, which was spoken by Phyllis, the lady who had escorted me in. She spoke about nice things. "Please look after the animal kingdom, and send healing to the four corners of the world." I remember thinking it was a strange phrase, given that the world is round, but I listened on. "...and please, God, protect us tonight as we link with the Spirit World."

"WHAT?! Protect us? From what?!" I screamed in my head. At that point I'd convinced myself that everything bad I'd heard about this place was true. It was a place for the devil, it must be, because if it wasn't then why do we need God to protect us? I was starting to sweat and nervously began to tap my foot, desperate to leave but at the same time not wanting to draw attention to myself. What on earth were these people going to do next?! The prayer came to an end and then the circle leader spoke again. "Sandra, could you see to the lights and the door, please?" Before she'd even finished her sentence, a small, birdlike woman quickly moved past me towards the door and, with a couple of clicks, switched off most of the lights and sealed my fate.

If I'd have been told that the lights would be turned off and the door would be locked I'm sure I would have been fine. As it was, I almost wet my pants and thought I was heading for the Spirit World that night! An anxiety was growing in me; I was feeling nauseous, frightened, trapped and with no means of escape. "How did I get myself into this situation? What was I thinking? I am never coming here again." These were the scared thoughts running through my frightened mind.

My eyes had adjusted to the semi-darkness when Phyllis got up. She walked slowly and determinedly in my direction, clasping her hymn-book. As she approached, I could feel my knuckles getting tighter and whiter and the sound of my own heartbeat filled my ears; I really didn't like this spiritualist stuff at all! As she got closer to me, she began to speak, thankfully in her own voice. "All I have to say to you, young man, is that you are very psychic and that within a year you will be standing here doing what I'm doing." She gestured towards the stage at the end of the church. "You see spiritual lights, don't you?"

I wanted to speak, but my mouth felt as if it was full of glue. I was aware that everyone in the room was looking at me, and suddenly, on top of everything else, I felt incredibly self-conscious, something I'd desperately wanted to avoid.

The pause after she'd spoken was long and tense; I really couldn't speak and my mind was racing, trying to process everything that had happened. On top of all that, the fear had really taken hold. In that moment I just nodded – it was all I was capable of. She could see I was overwhelmed and that I couldn't take in what else she was saying. I wasn't meaning to be rude – I couldn't speak to her at all; it was as if I had become detached from my own senses. I remember her final words to me as she came to the end of delivering her message: "Mark my words."

The fear in my mind had been replaced by a thousand and one questions. I was trying to make sense of what Phyllis had told me. How did she know that I saw lights? What made her say that one day I would stand on stage and do what she was doing? I had to stay and speak to her later that evening. I would never know anything about what I was seeing unless I spoke with her. That was the reason I was there in the first place and I wouldn't leave until I'd spoken with her.

The service was scheduled for an hour and I'd had enough excitement in that hour to last me a lifetime! The clock behind me said 7.50pm. Strangely, after the drama of the evening, I was now feeling completely relaxed and wasn't uncomfortable in any way. I was still observing everything, and I refused to close my eyes, in case I missed anything. Phyllis was still talking with the Spirit World and I was just taking it all in. She was speaking to a lady on the opposite side of the church and the message seemed to be coming to an end.

I was listening intently when a most significant event occurred that changed everything: I saw an image in front of me. My eyes were open and yet I could clearly see a face literally suspended in mid-air in front of me – no body, no arms or legs, just a face. The face belonged to a lady, and the odd thing was that I could only see half of it. It wasn't disfigured, there was no blood and it wasn't in any way gruesome. I could describe the colour of her hair, the shape of her face, her eye colour, her nose; it was as if she was standing directly in front of me, except I could only see half of her. I instinctively 'knew' that this lady connected to the woman Phyllis was speaking to. I focussed on it and took in every detail. Just as I was getting used to the image being there, it went. It was replaced by another image; this time the picture was of a tattoo on a man's forearm, his left forearm. It was in the shape of a ship's anchor, with the ring and the crown part of the anchor spanning his arm. The tattoo was light blue in colour and it had a chain wrapped around it. I could tell that the arm belonged to an older man – the skin seemed weather-worn and the image was so clear I could make out that the outline of the tattoo wasn't as sharp as it would have been when it was first done. Although I saw the two pictures separately, I strongly felt that the lady and the owner of the tattoo were somehow related. I didn't know how I knew that, I just did. That was it, nothing more. I sat there, motionless and without thought, waiting for something else to appear, but there was nothing.

Slowly my own thoughts started to return, only to be interrupted by the sound of the leader's voice: "Does anyone have anything else they'd like to give before we close the circle?"

This could be my chance to speak, to stand and deliver what I'd seen. Everyone else who had seen or heard something during the evening had stood up easily and just told the group what they'd experienced. They were met with various, 'yes's, 'no's, or 'I don't know's, but this didn't seem to deter people – they just kept standing up and delivering their messages. In a split second, I had decided I just couldn't do it – I was too shy, too scared and too new to even see anything, let alone say anything to anyone. I didn't understand what had happened and I didn't want to make a fool of myself trying to make sense of it either.

The service was brought to a close promptly at 8pm and most of the people stayed afterwards for a cup of tea and the chance to discuss the messages they had received. I sat on my own for a while, remembering what I had seen. It felt strange and at the same time it felt wonderful. Was it really spirits trying to contact their loved ones through me? It certainly didn't fit with how I thought the 'dead' would appear – not a ghostly mist in sight and thankfully nothing had floated or moved around the room. I had to find out whether what I had experienced was real or my imagination, so I approached the woman who seemed to be in charge of the circle.

Sheila explained that only seeing half of a face could mean that the lady had suffered a stroke before she had died, and that the tattoo probably belonged to someone in her family. She suggested that I should speak to the person whom I thought the message was for. She explained that it would be the only way to really find out whether it actually was a message or if what I had seen had come from my very active imagination.

I felt frightened all over again, but this was a different kind of fear; I was not scared of being in a spiritualist church this time. It wasn't because I could have actually been in touch with the spirit of a 'dead' person. No, this time I was frightened that the lady wouldn't be able to accept the message, that I had somehow got it wrong and that I had missed some important detail or that she'd think I was crazy. I wanted to run out of the place for the second time, but I couldn't get the pictures I had seen out of my mind – I had to speak with her.

She was a small person and was sitting with another lady who was later introduced to me as her sister. She wore lots of gold jewellery and spoke with a non-local accent. She was very friendly and invited me to sit with them. Mustering my courage, I explained to her what I had seen in as much detail as I could recall. I told her how I'd felt, how I knew the message belonged to her and related to her the explanation I had been given for what I had seen. I kept my eyes closed for most of it and when I got to the end of my speech I opened them, unsure of the reaction. The relief I felt was tangible; I felt as though a great weight had been lifted from my shoulders, and to my surprise, the lady confirmed to me that what I had seen was accurate. She spoke to me of how her grandmother had suffered a stroke just before her death and how, as a result of it, she had lost the use of one side of her face. Apparently, the description I offered of her grandmother was extremely accurate. The tattoo, she explained, was on her grandfather's left arm and that it was a ship's anchor because he was in the navy. She thanked me for the message and said she felt reassured that they were now together in the Spirit World; she said it gave her some peace. All it seemed to give me was a headache!

I hadn't told my parents that I was going to the Spiritualist Church. I knew that they would go crazy if I even suggested it, so I had told them I was visiting my friend Martin's house instead. I only intended going once anyway; I wanted to see what really went on, get the answers I wanted, leave, then never go again. There would be no point in telling them. "What they didn't know wouldn't hurt them," I thought. I convinced myself that it was OK to tell a lie about where I would be, but the spirit people clearly didn't.

In all the excitement of the evening, I had completely forgotten that on my way into the church, I had bought some raffle tickets. Apparently, the church survived on donations from the congregation and from the raffle that was drawn at the end of each service. I didn't even know what the prize was, but when I checked my tickets I had won! It was the first thing I had ever won and I was absolutely gutted. I had won a bottle of wine! How would I explain to my mum where it had come from? I was seventeen years old and I couldn't drink alcohol because of the medications I was on for the migraine. I also wasn't old enough to buy alcohol anyway and, besides, I had no reason to, nor did I have the money. Telling the truth about where the bottle came from also meant owning up to where I had been – don't you just hate being found out?

Being a rebellious teenager, I wouldn't give in. I'm an Aries and am typically stubborn. In my parents' eyes, spiritualism wasn't 'healthy', especially for a seventeen-year-old who had just left school to train to be an electrician, who had a career plan. To me, this need to visit the church was based on a strong feeling and most definitely not a 'phase'. The rebellious teenager in me decided that I would go anyway and lie about where I'd been. The truth about lying when you're seventeen is that people older than you usually see through it very easily, as did my parents. It wasn't helped by the fact that for the next twelve weeks, every Wednesday at 9pm I would walk in having won yet another raffle prize – clearly the Spirit World didn't like me lying about where I'd been, and I was too stupid to stop buying tickets after week two and was too excited to throw away the bottle of wine at the end of week one!

I don't remember exactly the moment when the 'discussions' about my new-found interest stopped; maybe it was when my parents realised that I hadn't turned into a dope-smoking hippie or that I hadn't been carried away to a cult gathering, never to be seen again. Maybe it was neither of those things, but rather a sense that I was happier in many ways since I'd started attending the Spiritualist Church. I had always been a quiet, reserved lad, under-confident and not at all comfortable being around people. I was a lonely child, anxious, and always felt on the periphery at school, and in some ways, though I was still very much Darren, I was now much more confident, happy and comfortable with who I was. I continued my studies at college, although I knew in my heart that being an electrician wasn't my calling in life;

and the fears my parents had about who and what I would become dissolved when they saw the effect that attending the Spiritualist Church appeared to have on me. I certainly did feel happier; there seemed to be a purpose to my life and, apparently, I was good at this mediumship thing.

People would tell me how much they felt helped by the messages I'd passed on to them in the weekly circle, and in turn, I felt even more of a need to be more accurate the following week. The feeling of self-confidence in me rocketed: I was more sociable, I felt content, I dressed in brighter clothes instead of the black I usually favoured and, more importantly, I had a greater awareness of the world around me instead of the limited one I'd had from my bedroom window for most of my teenage life.

Whilst I attended the circle every week, I didn't yet fully understand how I was able to speak with the Spirit World. Each week I just sat quietly in the circle, and I'd suddenly feel as if the space beside me had in some way been 'filled'. When I concentrated on the 'space', I would start to hear a voice, sometimes next to my right ear or sometimes in my head. I could tell whether the voice was male or female, sometimes even work out the age, and the more I listened, the more I was able to feel the emotions of the person communicating. Occasionally I saw the person speaking to me too, but I only ever saw them standing to the left of me and when I did they were often solid and not at all ghostly. "Weren't you scared when you first started hearing them?" is usually the first question that people ask when I tell them what I do, and I can honestly say that I wasn't. I quickly accepted that the people communicating to me were 'real' people, there was nothing remotely frightening about them and they were only ever loving in the way they spoke and gave me no reason to be scared. Sometimes I would just 'know' things, such as the name of someone's mum, or the number of children they had, without hearing or seeing a thing. It was as if a piece of information was 'dropped' into my head somehow and I knew it was relevant. Over a period of time, I became increasingly trusting of the information I received, more confident in standing up in front of people, and almost a year later, as predicted and yet completely unplanned, I found myself standing on platform, but not at all ready, to take my first demonstration.

CHAPTER 3

REALISATION

Freda, some forty years older than me, was my dearest friend from the church in Stainforth. We were total opposites, and yet the minute we met we just hit it off and seemed to bring out the mischief in each other. We always sat next to each other, and whether it was healing or a circle or a service, one or both of us usually ended up laughing so hard we couldn't breathe. It was hard not to laugh; we would always find something amusing, for example, the time she was told by a medium that one of her Spirit Guides was a dwarf, then, whilst I was giving healing to someone and trying to be serious, she decided to ask out loud whether she could now get on the bus for half price as a child fare! Freda was, and still is, a kind soul, one who puts others first and yet life hasn't been kind to her. Her most recent husband of only one year passed with a heart attack; she's experienced various family issues, relationship issues and the usual life experiences we all go through; but she has never indulged in self-pity. Freda embodies the true meaning of the word spiritual, although she's far too modest to admit that. On a Sunday afternoon we would often head out to the church in Warmsworth, which was on the opposite side of Doncaster from where we both lived. Unlike other churches, this one began their Divine Service at three in the afternoon.

From the outside the building was barely recognisable as a church at all and there was nothing to suggest anything spiritual happened in the place. It was made entirely of wood, and almost every panel showed signs of rot and damage. The smell of damp hung in the air, and when you walked in you would automatically want to cough. The church held no more than twenty people and every Sunday the place was full. There were times when we sat in prayer and I'd observe parts of the ceiling suddenly flaking off and landing in the neatly set hair of the congregation! Regardless of it being run-down, the smell and the risk of falling debris, the energy was alive. The minute you walked in, the hairs on the back of your neck stood up and it was like mini electric shocks nicely running down your back and arms. It was often said that the love inside the church kept it together, and because of this love, I had witnessed some amazing mediumship there.

This particular Sunday we didn't know the medium taking the service; we always went and just enjoyed being there, so it was sort of irrelevant who would take the meeting. We took our seats shortly before the start of the service, and suddenly I felt a rush of excitement. There was no real reason, but my stomach started to spin like Christmas was just around the corner. I'd mentioned to Freda how I felt and she suggested that maybe I was going to get a message from the visiting mediums – it was a possibility. I dismissed the feeling and started chatting to Freda about how eventually I might like to work on platform, although I felt I wouldn't get the opportunity and possibly not even like it when I was on the platform. I allowed myself to play the 'what if?' game in my head: "Imagine, standing up on the platform, with all those eyes looking at you, expecting, wanting, yearning for a connection from their loved ones and the pressure of needing to deliver – I can't imagine how that would feel?" I was anxious at the thought of it.

Freda was as reassuring as ever: "I think you could do it – you do really well in the circle, you've come on so quickly," she said, touching my arm. She smiled at me and checked her watch. "They're cutting it fine" she said. "It's ten minutes to go." She was looking towards the door.

I thought, "What if I were to get up there, couldn't deliver and then have to sit down again? God, I'd be mortified. People would think I was a fraud if I got it wrong." I found myself shaking my head at the thought of this possible scenario.

I'd been attending Divine Services for almost a year; I had witnessed so many mediums taking services and they always made it look easy. The very thought that I might be the demonstrating medium brought me out in a cold sweat. I reasoned that it was definitely a 'sign' that this wasn't for me. I'd been chasing my own thoughts now for far too long and had quickly decided that being a medium on a platform was definitely not for me – in future I'd stick to only working in the circle and dismissed any further thoughts about it. I'd made my decision. The finality of that thought brought me back to full awareness; I found that Freda was no longer sitting with me and was speaking to some recently arrived people. She was animated and smiling, and I could tell that she knew them well, although I'd never met them before. I caught her eye just as she pointed towards me; she gestured me over to speak with her friends and I was then introduced to Glen and Harry. I liked them immediately. Harry was a very tall, strong and imposing figure; he had a deep, rich voice which, although loud, was strangely calming. He was wearing a light grey suit, his slightly receding hair was brushed back and he wore dark-framed, square spectacles. He had the presence of someone whom you could trust; he felt dependable and, somehow, he made me feel safe.

Glen was an attractive woman in her late forties and she was very smartly dressed – easy to talk to, incredibly down to earth and I instantly liked her. What most struck me about her was that she had a sense of fun, her eyes twinkled and yet, when she spoke, she was really relaxed. I remember that she had looked at me strangely, almost like she was looking through me; she clearly knew something 'more' than she was letting on.

I was aware of the time and so I wished them both good luck, said how nice it was to meet them and started to gesture towards Freda to take our seats. It was then the bombshell dropped: "I've told them about you and they said they're happy for you to share the service with them," Freda explained. "I hope that's OK?"

What?! My stomach fell to the floor and my mind went into overdrive; there was no way that I felt ready for that! Every possible reason to *not* do it ran through my head in that moment, ranging from a conviction that I'd fail to feeling that I wasn't dressed properly and awareness that my hair needed cutting! None of the mediums were having any of those lame excuses, and so, with three pairs of eyes staring at me and a heavy, pregnant silence between us, I finally agreed to give it a try and had less than five minutes before we started the service. I went to the toilet to pray.

I sat there in a small toilet cubicle. There was something strangely comforting about being in such an enclosed space when I was feeling so very anxious. For the next few minutes I prayed, pleading with God to not let me fail. I also prayed that the audience would receive help, that I would also receive help and that He wouldn't let me vomit on anyone in the process! I prayed so hard that I bit my lip until it bled; the pain was so bad that it was hard to bring my awareness back to the people in the next room who were waiting for me to astound them and give life-changing messages. I tried to calm myself down and to focus – it was very difficult.

Sitting in the safety and comfort of an open circle was one thing – there was no pressure there; if mediumship happened then it did and if it didn't no-one was disappointed – but to have to stand up in front of unfamiliar people in a place I loved but had never worked in was another level of scary!

I unbolted the toilet door and nervously walked towards the church hall. I felt (and I'm sure I looked) like a condemned man. Why on earth had I agreed to this? The platform was tiny; it was barely big enough for two people, let alone a third person plus the chairperson, to sit comfortably. Somehow, we all squeezed on. I'd purposefully asked if I could sit on the end of the platform so I could make a quick exit, should it all go terribly wrong. Glen looked at me sympathetically and I took my seat. I remember the chairperson started by introducing Glen and Harry as the mediums for the service and then saying, "This is Darren from Stainforth Church – this is his first time on the platform so please send your love up to him." At that point my stomach flipped, but I faked a smile and closed my eyes. Harry then started the service with an opening prayer and both Freda and Glen were giving me encouraging smiles.

I'd love to be able to write more fully about exactly what happened from this point and in the order that things occurred, but I honestly have no memory of it. I had my eyes closed for most of the service and the only thing I remember being aware of was the movement of Glen and Harry as they got up to demonstrate. I'm unable to recall what they said exactly and to whom or even what was really going on within me. I *do* know it was late in the service when Glen finally turned to me and asked if I had anything I wanted to give – until then I must have totally zoned out.

As I nervously stood up, I heard a lady's voice from the Spirit World: "I'm her mum and she has my pearls – they're in her jewellery box on her dressing table." The voice directed me to a lady sitting at the back of the church. The message was for Barbara, the church secretary; she'd been selling raffle tickets when we arrived. I remember nothing else about the communication other than physically shaking all the way through it.

The hour had passed and the service came to a close. I had delivered one message and, thankfully, it had been accepted. The sense of relief was immense as I stepped off the platform and headed towards Freda for a cup of tea and a debrief. We chatted about it all the way home, and beyond all of the nervousness, the fear and the shock of actually being invited to share the service, I was so happy that I hadn't been let down by Spirit. God had heard me and answered my prayers, and I was so very grateful. Clearly God had also heard the conversation I had with Freda before the service and had decided it was time for me to experience being a medium on the church platform – He really was everywhere! I realised then just how powerful thoughts were. Literally minutes after asking, the experience I'd sought answers for had manifested. I had apparently delivered the message with such accuracy that it shook me, and this led me to the next phase of my spiritual unfoldment. It was almost exactly a year to the day that I had first visited the church in Stainforth where Phyllis delivered to me the message and as predicted, here I was, a medium on the platform.

CHAPTER 4

REALITY

"I wonder how it would feel?" is an innocent question. It is a question that doesn't really require an answer; it is just one of those questions we all ask ourselves on a daily basis in order to measure what we *might* feel in a particular situation. It was that particular question that ultimately led to me starting my life as a medium and demonstrating publicly. I'd always been told that thoughts are 'real and living things', that they have a power of their own; what we think is as powerful as the spoken word. Whether that thought is deemed positive or negative, the effects of these thoughts are very real and tangible. After all, if we sit and dwell on negative things, we will eventually feel the emotional and physical effects of those thoughts. I completely 'got' that; it was common sense to me. Also, in my limited understanding of how the Spirit World worked, everything came about as a direct result of our thoughts. I would simply think about communicating with the Spirit World, and almost immediately, the response to that thought *was* communication. I didn't particularly need to offer up a lengthy prayer, nor did I need to sit quietly for half an hour or chant whilst waving an incense stick! Clearly there was an intelligence outside of me, and all that was required to access it was for me to think a certain thought and wait.

What I didn't realise at that time was that *all* thoughts are 'heard' by the Universe and taken literally; even the 'I wonder how...' thoughts are seen by the Universe as an invitation to accommodate my desire for more understanding. Fortunately, the desire for more understanding was usually answered with an experience providing me with more insight into the situation. Everything I've ever needed to know in life has been brought to me through a person or an experience. The opportunity to stand on platform in Warmsworth was preceded by my initial 'I wonder how...' thought, and of course, the Universe inspired Freda to act and thereby manifest the experience.

Freda's husband, Fred, had passed away from a massive heart attack, having lived with a heart condition for many years. We were talking about it one day, and I remember thinking how awful it must have been for him to be aware that he had a problem and had no option other than to live with knowing that at any moment his life could change, or in fact end dramatically. It was something that I really couldn't comprehend, but I questioned how it might have felt for him. I couldn't imagine having to think that every day may be my last and there was nothing that could be done about it. Apparently, Fred had accepted this condition and the daily medication as part of his life and, such as he could, continued to live it.

A couple of weeks after the conversation about Fred, I'd started to experience breathlessness. Nothing major, and not constantly, but there were definitely times when it was more difficult to breathe than at others. I visited the doctor, who listened to my chest and mentioned that he could hear sounds which might indicate a heart murmur, and he requested further tests. It was an anxious time and one that reminded me of my earlier thought about 'I wonder how...' The scan of my heart took place three weeks later and thankfully everything was fine, but for three weeks I had experienced the anxiety of what *might* be. Ironically, when Fred eventually passed away his ashes were scattered in the grounds of the new church in Warmsworth after the original church was taken down.

It was exactly the same scenario with my dad's appendix operation. He was ill with appendicitis and eventually his appendix burst leading to peritonitis, a potentially life-threatening infection in his abdomen. One day we were discussing it, and whilst listening to his story, my very inquisitive mind innocently thought, "I wonder how..." As with Fred, I couldn't imagine just how awful it would be to have your appendix infected and be so ill that you might die suddenly. Again, two weeks later the exact same thing happened. I was on my way home from my grandparents' house and developed a severe stomach ache. Twenty-four hours later I was in hospital recovering from an operation to remove my appendix, which had literally burst just as the surgeon had started to remove it. By this time, you would have thought I'd have 'got the hint' and made the link between thought and experience, but no, I'm a little slow sometimes at putting two and two together, and the final experience literally changed my understanding of the principle of 'cause and effect'.

I loved to watch *The Oprah Winfrey Show*. She was a pure inspiration to me and I found her brand of TV enlightening and profoundly healing, not only to the guests on her show, but I also felt sure it was healing for the viewing audience as well. One of her programmes, which highlighted the effects of gun crime, featured a young man. He lived in the Bronx in New York, an area where gun crime was rife, and as I watched him tell his story I was transfixed. This poor man had been walking home from work when someone had leaned out of a car with apparently no motive and shot him in the knee, shattering it completely. The man was left disabled from the incident and not just with physical scars. I was incredibly touched by his story and shocked at such behaviour. I thought about his story and once again, attached the 'I wonder how...' thought before it.

A few days after seeing the programme, I'd done a demonstration at my local Spiritualist Church and was making the short walk home afterwards. I crossed the bridge between the next village and my home when I heard shouts from behind me. I couldn't fully make out what was being shouted; I was initially startled by the sound and thought it was some youths joking around on the steps beside the bridge. I turned around to see what was happening and saw a white Ford Escort van speeding towards me. I could see two people in the van and on the passenger side, there was a man partly leaning out of the window, pointing what looked to me like an air rifle. I was stunned and literally froze on the spot. By this time the van was no more than six feet away and it felt like time was standing still, and yet it could only have been a matter of three seconds from hearing their shouts to them being in front of me. The man was dark haired, his skin looked weather-worn, he was in his early twenties and he was wearing a white polo neck shirt with the collar turned up. I watched him steady the rifle by resting it on the bottom of the window – he appeared to be trying to fix it on me – all the time he was still shouting words I couldn't make out and laughing. I then heard it: a bang; it wasn't a huge noise, more like the crack of a whip, but I knew that the gun had been fired. I jumped back towards the wooden fence and watched the van speed along the road. I was feeling too shocked and frightened to take note of the registration number.

I watched the van speed away and saw the rifle retract, and the window go up. It was then that I felt a sharp, piercing, stinging pain – not at all what I imagined being shot would feel like. My immediate reaction was to discover the source of the pain and so I slowly lifted my left trouser leg, which was now sporting a hole where the pellet had penetrated. My knee looked pretty normal apart from a small, reddened area just under the knee cap. I wasn't in a huge amount of pain at this point – I felt more in shock than anything else – and the wound the pellet had left was only bleeding slightly. It was as I rolled down my trouser leg that I realised that while it was a different gun, and probably different motivation and thankfully a very different outcome, it was significant enough to remind me of my response to the man's story on *The Oprah Winfrey Show*.

'Be careful what you wish for' was a phrase I'd heard many times and given little heed to, along with other similar phrases. Old wives' tales I'd thought were just mumbo jumbo, not at all based on reality and attitudes belonging to a different generation to mine. And yet, in the space of a couple of months, I had directly experienced the power of my own thoughts in action, literally what I gave out as a thought, came back to me. I didn't *think* I was asking for them. I had merely tried to understand more fully the pain of another person's experience and, without realising it, somehow 'activated' the power that manifested opportunities to offer me a greater understanding.

Now I'm not suggesting that you should avoid trying to understand others' pain; nor am I suggesting that if you do, you will always manifest the exact same experience within and around you. What I *am* suggesting is that we are capable of manifesting our thoughts into reality through the power of intent and desire. Whether those thoughts are conscious or unconscious, the Universe has to honour what we wish for ourselves; whatever we focus on will manifest. I had wished for a greater understanding of those situations, and because my belief is that to know anything I must experience it first, the Universe gave to me what I'd asked for in ways most appropriate to my choice of learning.

There have been many instances over the years, similar to those I have related that have left me in no doubt of the power and presence of the Universe. Those same experiences have shown me how connected we are to everything in the Universe and also how benevolent and kind it is too; some of those experiences have been incredibly positive and inspiring – it wasn't all illness and gunshots!

Many years later, I recall an incident after I had made the decision to become a full-time medium. I wasn't feeling particularly well that day; I was tired and had been burning the candle at both ends. I was demonstrating a couple of times a week and doing private sittings as well as working at a full-time job – I was exhausted. I wasn't eating properly either, just grabbing what I could, and was basically ignoring all the signs that I needed to rest. I was sitting in the bath, thinking about how terrible I felt and how I needed to nurture myself more and implement a healthier diet. As I sat there soaking, I came up with an 'action plan' of how to get myself into better shape in body and mind. It started with making some good, nutritious food. Once out of the bath and feeling motivated, I checked the freezer and cupboards only to find that I hadn't got any of the ingredients I needed; I made a mental list and headed back upstairs to get dressed, deciding I'd pick them up in town later. I was just finishing getting ready when the doorbell rang; it was my friend June holding a foil-covered dish with a big smile on her face;

"I made some shepherd's pie yesterday and made too much, I wonder if you and Chris would eat it?" She motioned the dish towards me and I invited her in whilst excitedly explaining my plan for the day and what I'd decided whilst sitting in the bath. She stayed for a coffee and then shortly after I left to go into town. I had a couple of errands to make, one of which was to check my bank account, and I also needed to pick up my P45 from my last employer.

Now, I don't like having any kind of debt, and so when the numbers on the screen at the cash machine said that I owed the bank £166.36, I wasn't a happy Darren. Slightly disgruntled, I reasoned with myself that maybe I would have people call up for sittings that week so I could pay it back –

I wouldn't be in debt for long. Plus, at least I didn't need to spend money on food now as I had shepherd's pie, which would probably last us for a couple of days at least; that thought somehow made things feel easier.

I made my way from there into the opticians, my former place of work, to collect my last payslip and P45. I stood talking to the girls about the pie that had arrived that morning as I opened the slip. My boss had already told me that I was probably due a tax refund but said it would likely come through after I'd left the company, so I wasn't hopeful of receiving it any time soon. I looked at the figures, not fully understanding the details on the slip, until I got to the part marked 'refund'. There, in black and white, was the total refund to be paid to me: *exactly* £166.36, *exactly* the same amount I had been concerned at owing to the bank, having found out about the debt less than twenty minutes before! The feeling of gratitude was overwhelming at that point as I recalled again the earlier events of the day. I was amazed that not only had the Universe known I needed to buy food, they sent it via June, *and* the exact meal I was planning to make. It also knew my feelings about debt, and there, right in front of me, was the exact amount of money I'd owed – even better was that it was to be credited to my account the following day! Really, this was miraculous!

I'd been chatting for about thirty minutes, about all manner of things relating to work and also organising my leaving meal with my former colleagues. It was then that I had an uncomfortable feeling. I say it was a feeling, but I couldn't give it a name; it was more of a knowing. Whatever it was, it literally stopped me mid-sentence and the pull inside me was so strong; I needed to go home, there and then, right now! There was no mistaking it for something else; my instinct was screaming to go home right now, and even though I didn't understand why, I daren't NOT listen to it in light of the events of the day so far. I made my excuses and quickly left the shop. I hurried home, trying to work out what the impulse could be about. Ten minutes later, I arrived home and opened the back door to be greeted by a strange smell. I wasn't familiar with the smell and it certainly wasn't a pleasant one either. I placed my bag down and went into the living room, eager to find out not only what the smell was but also why I had felt such urgency to get home.

As I walked through the door, a most noxious smell rushed out to meet me and there was a loud cracking noise. I turned to the direction of the sound only to see the mantelpiece light up in bright flash of orange light! I then realised what was happening. In all the excitement of seeing June, I'd forgotten to blow out the candle under the oil burner before I'd left for town. Somehow the bowl had cracked and it looked like the oil inside it was now on fire, flames licking against the wallpaper and dark wisps of smoke hanging in the air. I rushed back into the kitchen and grabbed a dishcloth, ran it under the tap and covered the burner, then carried it outside, coughing all the way. I then returned to the living room to inspect the damage and thankfully there was very little: only slight soot damage on the wallpaper where the flames tried to climb up the wall and that was all. The smell lingered for a while but nowhere near as much as the memory of what could have happened had I ignored that pull to go back home.

We only ever really need to ask the Universe to assist us with something once, and then *allow* it to meet our request. In fact, it knows what we need before we do, but adding our voice to our desire sets the Universe into action. This isn't as easy as it sounds, but knowing ourselves inside and out will help us to understand more clearly what role our conscious and unconscious thoughts play in creating our lives. We tend to spend so much time fighting to be heard in this world there is an automatic assumption that we have to keep asking and praying for something we'd like, behaving like a small child nagging their parents constantly until their needs are met. Usually when our request doesn't show up as we expect it to, or at all, we just keep asking, usually more loudly, and more often. We ask others their opinions and sometimes we ask them to help us. We sometimes seek out a psychic or a medium, and we ask them the same questions or ask them to make predictions for us about when and how our heart's desire will manifest. When it *still* doesn't show up, we entertain the idea of finding some kind of church to visit, believing that our plea will carry more weight on sacred ground. Sometimes we even light a candle, write in a prayer book and then finally, when all else seems to fail, we bargain. We make promises about what we'll do, say or be, if only we could get what we want 'just this once'. Or maybe I'm just speaking about myself? I was guilty of being this kind of person back then, and I still can be now too, albeit to a much lesser degree. Whilst I still do love to sit in a church, or any place of worship, I now know it isn't the *place* which activates the prayer, nor is it the method or process of prayer or its delivery; it's the intention and the prayer itself. I *AM* the sacred ground where all prayers are heard and I pray several times daily. I pray as a way of aligning my mind with the Divine Mind and to be in harmony with the Source of All that is. I pray to receive guidance, I pray for support, I pray for others and I pray to be in alignment with that force because I know that anything I ask of God *has* to show up in a godly way.

These early experiences of 'like attracts like' and 'ask and it's given' made me look seriously at whether I was somehow attracting, creating and inviting things to come to me. If I accepted that life was reflecting my thinking, and it certainly seemed to be, then could it also reflect other aspects of me – my beliefs, my words and my emotions – too? If that *were* true, then this was huge, because it would mean that as a medium receiving information from the Spirit World, what they communicated could possibly be because of a similarity they had with me, or it could be due to an expectation I held about them? Could it be possible that they recognised something about my life or the people I knew that was similar to their own life experience? I had noticed that when I demonstrated there were times when I believed that my mind was interfering. Sometimes I'd suddenly see an image of my grandad, or my mum's name would jump into my mind. I assumed that because of tiredness, or lack of focus, I'd unwittingly allowed my link with the Spirit World to drop, therefore letting my own thoughts and memories to surface. I'd also noticed that sometimes the messages or the people communicating from Spirit seemed to be similar as well. It frustrated me, and I blamed myself totally.

By this time, my experiences as a medium had made me very clear about the purpose of mediumship, both for the communicator and for the recipient. I could assess the benefit of spirit communication through the reactions of the spirit and the recipient and could also see the value of it. Mediumship really does have a therapeutic benefit. Simply delivering what I received now wasn't enough, though; I wanted more fully to study and explore the experience of mediumship within *me* as the medium. I wanted to understand whether parts of me or my experiences are 'useful' to the Spirit World and why; was there a connection between who I am as a person and the kind of medium that makes me? I wanted to explore the *process* of mediumship as well as experiencing different aspects of it.

CHAPTER 5

THE PROCESS

From my own experiences, I had established that there appeared to be a process I went through to achieve connection with the Spirit World. The process relied heavily on reducing my awareness of the physical world and instead focussing my awareness more onto my feelings, whilst observing the thoughts that came into my mind. Whether I wanted to use my psychic faculty, my ability to access inspirational speech, or to connect for healing mediumship or evidential mediumship, the process was the same, but with differing levels of depth and involvement.

When we die, the physical body is the only part of us that dies. Everything that makes up the Spirit World is non-physical. It is energy, thought and ether. Therefore, it made sense to me that when, through our psychic or mediumistic awareness, we have an experience from the Spirit World, then because the communicator in Spirit isn't physical, our awareness of them can't be through the physical senses either.

In my early spiritual development, I had expected that when I heard a voice from Spirit, I would hear it with my physical hearing. I also believed that if I were to see someone, then I would see them with my physical eyes, so I would discount any kind of awareness that didn't meet my own expectations. The truth is that, with the exception of physical mediumship, all of our intuitive, psychic and mediumistic awareness comes through the feeling state; for years I'd been looking in the wrong place!

On my very first visit to the Spiritualist Church in the open circle, I'd noticed that the majority of people there sat with their eyes closed, their hands on their knees with their palms facing upwards. At the time it seemed that this was what people had to do to receive communication with the Spirit World. I was told that closing our eyes focussed our awareness within, and that holding our palms open and upward suggested that we were open and ready to receive. In retrospect, when I saw the very first images of the tattooed arm and lady's face, my eyes were fully open and my arms were crossed across my chest almost defensively, completely contradicting what I was seeing around me. This alone showed me that regardless of whether my eyes were open or shut and regardless of how I sat, the only relevant parts in contacting the Spirit World related to where my attention and awareness was being directed in that moment. I soon realised that the key to shifting my focus towards the Spirit World was that I had to completely move away from the influence of my physical senses in order to begin the process of connection, and I wanted to test that theory.

Mediums are often given bad press from the media, psychologists, magicians and others who tell us that we're not psychic at all and that all we're doing is reading body language. They claim we're reading and interpreting the body postures, positions and poses as manifestations of a person's inner world, and we're just particularly sensitive or perceptive to those signals. For example, if someone comes into the room for a private sitting and they're crying, you don't need to be a psychic to know they're upset. You can make all manner of assumptions about the reason behind their tears and some of those assumptions could be right, and others not so. The way they stand, the way they cover their bodies with their arms, the way they hang their head can all be suggestive of their inner pain and emotion, but unless they speak directly to us about the cause of their tears we really are none the wiser.

Whilst I'm not an expert on body language, I can completely accept that our bodies can and do indicate our emotional state, but is it possible for them to also communicate such specific information about our loved ones who have passed away too? Thinking of the person crying, can their body language alone tell us that they're crying because their eighteen-year-old son David died on a motorcycle on 21 April and that his mother had just placed his favourite sweets on his grave to mark his birthday? I'm prepared to be proved wrong on this, but I don't believe body language can communicate this level of detail. However, I know from experience that mediumship can and does provide this level of detail. What reading body language *does* give to us as mediums, however, is the ability to orientate our approach to a fragile person, to be sensitive to what they're feeling, and to sense what they're capable of receiving through our psychic and mediumistic connections.

Parkgate Spiritualist Society was a small church just on the outskirts of Rotherham in South Yorkshire. It was run at the time by a lady called Pat Gamston, who was fierce in her defence of good-quality mediumship and also in the progression of spiritualism. After each of my many demonstrations at the church, it was customary for us to have long conversations on all manner of spiritual subjects; these often went on well into the night. One evening I remember we were speaking about ways in which we could strengthen our connections with Spirit and we agreed it was disappointing that some mediums seemed to focus so intently on the recipients of the communication that they abandoned their connection to the Spirit World. We'd both observed that some mediums were so focussed on the recipient that perhaps all they were doing was reading the signals from the recipient's body language, rather than receiving clear evidence from the Spirit World. During the conversation, I flippantly said, "Blindfold 'em, see how it works then!" And then we stared smiling at each other as the imaginary light bulb went on above each other's heads! Before I'd left that evening, we'd made a date for me to take a demonstration of blindfold mediumship, primarily as a means of challenging myself, but also as a way to help me to understand my process a little more.

A few months later, while feeling extremely anxious, I arrived to demonstrate at 'An experimental evening of blindfold mediumship with Darren Brittain.' I'd already pre-agreed with Pat that I was to arrive before the church opened and she would whisk me into the speakers' room. There my mobile phone was removed; I was given headphones with music playing. The committee were also given strict instructions not to enter the room at all until I was to start the demonstration. I was told that if I needed the bathroom, I was to knock on the inside of the door, blindfold myself and then wait to be taken to the outside toilet. Pat had decided that I wasn't allowed to see who was escorting me and they weren't allowed to speak to me either. She had also explained that once I'd started the demonstration, the recipients weren't allowed to respond directly to me; only the chairperson could reply on their behalf so I couldn't hear their voice. They were only allowed to nod or shake their head in response as to whether the information was correct or not, and the chairperson would then tell me. She was taking this 'let's be sure it's Spirit' experience way too far, I thought!

All too soon, my prayers for assistance were interrupted by a very loud knock on the door and the headphones were removed. I felt my arm being firmly grasped and I was led, blindfolded, through the heavy door, feeling nauseous, fearful and yet again wondering what on earth I'd let myself in for. It was really happening! I stumbled up the wooden steps, holding the handrail, and my upper arm was still being gripped by the invisible person beside me. At the top of the steps, I was turned around by my escort and was slowly manoeuvred into my seat on the rostrum. The noise of the audience was louder than I'd expected. I tried to convince myself it was because I'd been wearing headphones, rather than because it was a packed room full of those waiting to see me fail. My heart was pounding and the reality of the situation hit me like a brick; the desire to rip off the blindfold and apologise was stronger than ever. I really didn't want to go through with it. I felt sure I must have forgotten to breathe; my chest felt completely constricted and my thoughts were more jumbled than ever.

I felt really nauseous and I began to wonder how I'd manage to leave the platform if I needed to vomit. I would have to take the blindfold off and then the evening would have to be cancelled completely. It was then I heard a voice in my mind. "Just breathe," it said. It was an unfamiliar, gentle voice; I couldn't even be sure of its gender. I focussed on my breath and managed to hold my attention on breathing for a moment when I was interrupted by the chairperson's introduction.

"...it'll be a wonderful evening guaranteed to show you all not only the intelligence of the Spirit World but also the level of trust that Darren has in them." At that point I admit that my thoughts weren't particularly spiritual or kind, and if I could have seen the chairman I'd have taken steps to silence him. I couldn't handle any more pressure than I already felt in that moment. The gentle voice in my mind spoke again. "Just breathe. Notice the pause between breathing out and breathing in." I listened intently and did as the voice suggested, partly through fear that if I didn't I'd fail, and partly in the hope that if I did, I'd somehow be alright. I found the pause; I'd never noticed there was one before, but it clearly separated the out breath and the in breath. This beautiful voice then spoke again. "The pause is where the stillness lives," it said. "Where does the pause live in your body?" My stomach, it was definitely in my stomach! I watched for the pause for a few more breaths to be certain it was still there, and as I did so, I became less and less aware of what was going on in the church around me. The voice spoke for a final time. "Imagine a light in your stomach and with every breath out, imagine you're making it bigger." The sense of calm was palpable and yet there was the indescribable feeling of the Spirit World around me like I had never experienced before. The space around me was full of their presence and I'd gone beyond feeling anxious and felt ready to do the demonstration.

In front of me was a barrier, which I held on to when I stood up, and as the demonstration progressed, I had to let go and started to pace up and down which was my usual practice. I had no anxiety about the demonstration, nor did I have fear of falling either; in fact, apart from the blindfold, it was business as usual. The chairman pointed out afterwards that there were times I came very close to the edge of the rostrum and he was ready to spring into action to save me if necessary, but the Spirit World prevented any mishap. Even now as I write this I can still remember one vivid image I saw in my mind during the demonstration. I'd come to the end of one communication and was trying to place the recipient for the last message of the evening. Now at that time, when trying to place the communication, sometimes I would clearly feel drawn to someone and instantly feel the Spirit World draw closer to me, and at other times I wouldn't know who the message was for at all. When that occurred, as each piece of evidence was delivered, it was a process of elimination, and eventually there would be only one person in the room who could understand all the information, thereby establishing that they were the correct recipient.

On this occasion, in my mind I clearly saw a woman in her mid-fifties with blonde hair; she was wearing a bright red coat with shiny red buttons. It was a military-style jacket with a high collar – quite stylish, I thought – and whilst I saw it in my mind's eye, it was slightly to the left of me and in the distance. I described what I'd seen as clearly as I could, and this was met with almost complete silence from the audience, apart from a few shuffling noises that I'd interpreted as signs that I'd failed. I stood there, trying not to overthink it, so I repeated the information again; this time I counted the buttons and remember saying, "It's a double-breasted jacket, and on the front, there should be six buttons in total, but the second button down on the left side is missing." I pointed to the area of the room where I had seen it in my vision, towards the back and to the left. It was then that I heard the chairperson speak more than the 'yes' and 'no' he'd been instructed to reply with that evening. "It's you! The woman at the back with the red coat on!" he shouted. It was met with a huge, irritated groan from the audience – irritation at the recipient for taking so long to acknowledge the description. I admit I was confused about what was happening; I thought I was describing a person in the Spirit World, but it turns out I was describing exactly the clothes of the recipient – a description that my physical eyes couldn't see but my inner vision saw, right down to the missing button!

After a very brief communication to the 'lady in red', the end of the evening arrived and I was finally allowed to remove the blindfold I'd been wearing for almost two and a half hours. I went back into the speakers' room where Pat arrived with tea. "I think that proved the point, don't you?"

she said with a grin on her face. The point being, it's not necessary for the medium to see the recipient at all to deliver the communication. In fact, in some cases it's beneficial to not look at them too much and instead to keep the focus on the Spirit World.

What I learned the most from the experience that night at Parkgate, was that the more I took the focus away from my physical senses, the more real the Spirit World became. It was like going inward, going deeper into my feelings and becoming less aware and affected by what was going on outside me. I think it's entirely understandable that by temporarily removing my physical sight, I became anxious, even more so when the purpose of the demonstration was to 'test' my awareness in a very public arena. What fascinated and educated me at the same time was that without putting on the blindfold, and without hearing that calming voice, I couldn't have even started to make the journey to the Spirit World that night. It certainly wasn't a voice I'd heard before and until that point I was still very much in my own head and fears; I'd only become aware of the Spirit World after I'd followed the voice's instructions. So, who was it? And where was it?

§

Instinct. Intuition. Higher self. Spirit. Hunch. Gut feeling. Inkling. That wise, kind, loving and knowing part of us is called by many different names; it is often ignored, but it is usually right. My intuition had led me to go home just in time to prevent the house catching fire and at that time it had come as a feeling. It was a similar sensation to when I was driving along the motorway and all of a sudden, I had an inescapable urge to change lanes only seconds before a sheet of ice flew off the top of the lorry in front of me. Had I not moved, it would have landed directly where I had just been. Call it what you will, I had learned that night in Parkgate that the wise part of me doesn't just speak in feelings; it can also present as a voice. I now recognise that voice as the voice of inspiration. The Merriam-Webster dictionary definition of inspiration states:

> "A divine influence or action on a person believed to qualify him or her to receive and communicate sacred revelation."

A 'divine influence' suggested that this voice came from a place of good and that it had my best interests at heart; after all, something divine to me meant of God. It also communicated something to me that I couldn't have known in any other way, certainly not with my physical senses. But more importantly, the voice soothed me, calmed me and enabled me to connect with the Spirit World, and that was a sacred revelation. Without the voice, I could not have so effectively bridged the gap between my own mind and the mind of those in the Spirit World. What I've come to realise because of that is how we connect to the Spirit World outside us. It really starts with acknowledging that we are already Spirit, here and now. The acknowledgment that we are indeed Spirit and that we come from the divine, the Universe or any other term you wish to use, means that we are ALL connected to each other and are therefore sensitive to each other once we identify with that intuitive and inspired part of us. We know things because we're connected. We know when our children are in danger because of that connection. We know when to make or take the call because we're connected to the person and therefore to their situation. We know when to change lanes, go home, reach out, be still or do nothing because that wise, loving, benevolent and divine part of us knows what is right, necessary and good for us; even if our ego, our will or our logic suggests an alternative. I like to think of it as the 'Sat Nav of the Soul'. It is the part of us that holds divine information, which is released when required, its purpose being to guide us, to show us the way and also to tell us when we've made a wrong turn. If we listen to it and follow its guidance, we're usually safer, we are protected and, more importantly, we are operating from a place of trust. If we ignore it, often in some way there is a negative consequence that comes from ignoring our inner voice. I'm sure we've all at some point ignored the sat nav, assuming that we know better, only to end up down a dead end, or in the wrong town, or on a dirt track up a mountain, feeling stressed, defeated and upset!

It's fascinating to me that if you ask a sceptical person whether they have any psychic ability, they would probably deny it because it goes against their logic, culture, religion, intellect, rationale or belief system. They will, however, usually accept that sometimes they have experienced a strong instinct, gut feeling or a 'knowing' about something which they have at some point in their lives listened to, followed or even possibly ignored. People have different names for the same phenomenon.

§

When we identify with the spiritual nature of ourselves and we use that sensitivity in service of, or in relation to, another, we call it being psychic. When we focus on a person and we really listen to our feelings in their presence, we can get a glimpse into their experience of life. Psychics aren't just able to receive information about people, though; we're also able to tune in to and interpret information about places and things. Long-distance events, experiences from the past, receiving information from objects, which it's claimed 'hold' on to the energy of the wearer, as well as finding missing people, are all made possible by accessing that inherent sensitivity. There's a saying that 'all mediums are psychic, but not all psychics are mediums'. What it means is that the ability to feel is inherent within everyone, we're all sentient beings and we all have a soul, which is where that awareness originates. It's very possible for a highly sensitive psychic to read the memory of a person's losses and grief without actually communicating with the person who has died. I've met some psychics who are frightened by the thought of communicating with the so-called 'dead', and I've also met many so-called 'mediums' who are actually just very good psychics who don't know they're not in direct communication with a passed loved one because they don't understand the nature of their own awareness.

One of the most profound experiences I'd had while working with my psychic faculty was uninvited and came completely out of the blue – thankfully it had a very positive outcome.

A young boy, around nine or ten years old, lived nearby in the village I grew up in. He was a quiet boy – so quiet, in fact, that in the three or so years he lived there, I'd never actually seen him speak. He would usually be playing alone, and although I'd sometimes see him with his sister and parents, he seemed to live in his own world and didn't appear to have any friends of his age. I remember always feeling a little sad when I saw him, as he reminded me a little of myself at that age: quiet, nervous and shy around people. I would usually smile at him when I did see him, but the smile was never returned, as he was clearly uncomfortable around others. I never tried to speak with him when I saw him; I remember all too well the discomfort of feeling forced to speak to the 'grown-ups' at that age myself. There were rumours in the village that his parents were having a difficult time – it was said by those who knew the family that there was alcohol involved, that the environment was 'toxic' and that it was 'no place for children.' It was also rumoured that this lad couldn't actually speak at all and that he had learning difficulties, although I never found out whether any of this was true. This made me feel even more aware of how isolated this little boy must have felt if it were true and my heart went out to him.

In the height of summer one day, the sun was shining and all seemed well, when suddenly there were screams which must have been heard streets away. This little boy's name was being shouted loudly by his mum. Even though I was indoors, I could tell there was panic in her voice – first hers and then his dad's. The screams intensified and became louder as they approached my parents' home. I ran to look through the window and saw that his parents were manically running up and down the street, banging on doors and stopping people to ask if they'd seen anything. There were cries of, "Where are the police?" and one by one, people came out of their homes to find out what was happening and to see if they could help. My mum went out too, and after a short time returned to explain what was happening.

Apparently the little boy had gone missing; he had been outside playing on his own and didn't come in at the time he was told to. An hour had passed and then another, and his mum, feeling more and more panicked and fearing he'd been taken by someone, had eventually called the police. As I went outside, like everyone else I felt anxious too, not only at the thought of what might have happened to this poor little boy that I felt a connection to, but also at seeing the fear and distress of his family. Finally, police cars arrived and by then the whole of the street was out, searching and asking questions to establish whether anyone had seen him and if so, when. By this time his mum was screaming at a police officer, "Why aren't you looking for him?" and was banging on his chest whilst his colleague was trying to calm her. I felt overwhelmed by the scene and incredibly powerless. The look of sheer desperation on his mum's face is something I can still clearly recall. I was searching my own memory and concluded that I hadn't actually seen the little boy that day, which was unusual as most days I did.

I went inside and wondered where he could have gone. Like his parents and neighbours, I feared the worst might have happened to him. It had been over two hours since he'd been seen by anyone and apparently it wasn't like him to not come back when called. It was then I wondered whether there was any way I might be able to feel where he could be by using my awareness. I remembered reading about a psychic many years before called Nella Jones, who had apparently helped the police to find Peter Sutcliffe, who was known more widely in the media as the Yorkshire Ripper, guilty of many murders committed in West Yorkshire in the 1980s. I felt it was worth a try and so I sat in the armchair and focussed. I didn't know what could happen, if anything, and I didn't even know how I should begin. I remember seeing Nella in a TV interview stating that she needed to hold an object to make a link to the victim – sometimes it was an item of their clothing. I didn't have anything of his I could hold, but I did have the feeling within me of a connection to him, so I focussed on that feeling instead. I brought to my mind the image of him: his short blond hair, his blue eyes, his build and the way he'd look away when I'd smile at him. I remembered the last time I'd seen him walking his green bike past my parents' house. I focussed, all the time thinking, "Where are you?", "What's happened?" It was then I felt that all my senses were suddenly alive and were filled with information.

The smell of the wood and varnish is filling my nose, it's making me feel sick and my left arm is in pain. I'm on the floor surrounded by wooden furniture and it's really dusty; my jeans are dirty and I know my mum won't like that and that I'm probably going to get into trouble for it. Both of my knees are bent and I'm crouched down, nestled into the corner with a window above me to my left. My left arm is pulled behind me and my shoulder is against the wall, which feels warm because the sun is shining onto it. My other arm is across my stomach and I can't move it either. Under the weight against my chest I can feel my heart racing and I can hear voices in the distance shouting, screaming my name. I want to shout back, but I can't, the words just won't come out. I'm feeling really tired, but I can't fall asleep and I know I shouldn't either – I need to keep trying to move. I don't know how long I've been in here and I'm feeling terrified and very alone. The heat in the room is making me feel funny, I'm thirsty, and my lips are feeling dry and scratchy too. I can only move my head to the right and as I turn it I can see the light of the sun shining in front of me. The wood is making funny shadows on the floor and I think some of them look like animals. There are sounds of wood clicking and creaking all around me and I feel really scared – what if I can't get out and no-one finds me?

That was it. As I came back to my own senses it felt clear to me that he was trapped somewhere. I was frantically trying to think of anywhere I'd been or seen used to keep wood. I knew from the visions I'd had that wherever he was, he was close enough to hear his mum's shouts, and so as I stood up to go outside, I said out loud, "GUIDE ME." The response was immediate – it was a pull, like something had been hooked on to me and was now reeling me in. My mind was still trying to make sense of what it had seen and I was trying to remember anywhere in the area that might match the description. It was a hot day and the heat of the sun could be felt clearly on my bare arms as I felt pulled down my garden by this invisible force. I remember thinking that if I was hot and could move around, and if what I'd experienced was actually his experience, then he was in trouble, because he couldn't move and was already feeling unwell. I'd considered telling the police officers what I'd seen, but I knew that I couldn't waste any time and instead I would follow this feeling to wherever it took me. I reasoned with myself that if I found nothing THEN I would tell them.

I was drawn into our back garden, somehow feeling guided along the patio onto the lawn beyond. I stopped for a moment, trying to feel where this force wanted to take me. I felt the direction change, I turned to the left and once more the feeling became stronger. It was like following an invisible trail, a trail I could only feel using my non-physical senses. I was pulled towards the neighbour's garden and I climbed the fence, not at all concerned that they wouldn't approve of me invading their territory. It's odd to say that the feeling got somehow thicker the more I followed it, but it did. As I climbed the fence and planted my feet on the grass on the other side of it, the pull became the only thing I could focus on. I was drawn towards a house down the street. I walked slowly towards it, feeling increasingly aware that the poor little boy was feeling trapped, scared and in pain, but also mindful that I had to make sure I didn't lose touch with this feeling. It was then the feeling changed. It was no longer just a feeling, but it became much more physical for me.

A strange vibration started to run through my body, a shaking sensation as though every part of me was being electrified. I knew that this particular neighbour was a bit of a hoarder – his garden was always full of what I thought was junk, bits of old lawnmowers, garden tools and goodness knows what else. I was also aware of my own anxiety as I stood looking at his property, because as a child this neighbour called the police on me and my brother for nailing a makeshift tent to his fence. I had always felt him to be unstable. The strength of the vibration brought my awareness back to why I was standing there. As I looked to my left I could see the street was starting to fill with more people and more police; at that point a van marked 'Dog Unit' went past the entrance of the gate. "This is really serious," I thought. As I looked to my right I was looking down the neighbour's garden, which was planted with potatoes and onions, and I could see the cane framework for runner beans covered in bright green foliage and orange flowers. I turned my head back, and in front of me to my left was the back door and to the right of it, along from the kitchen, stood a makeshift shed. The shed had been made from old window frames, and a battered old door marked the entrance and also seemed to hold everything else in place. The vibration within me at this point was stronger than ever; it was pulling me towards the door. I felt fearful and hopeful at the same time – a strange combination, I thought, as I placed my hand on the doorknob. I was struck by how cold it felt given how hot the day was, but I turned it to the left and gently pushed it open. It can't have moved more than a couple of inches before it seemed to hit something behind it which stopped the door opening any further. I could see through the window that the place was jammed with all manner of things, so it was no surprise that this was as far as the door could open. I felt deflated; the opening of the door wasn't wide enough to allow anyone through it – it was no more than three inches wide – so I reasoned that he couldn't have got in there. I looked through the window again in all directions, but there was no sign of him – clearly my feeling was wrong.

I stepped back from the shed feeling confused and disappointed, and turned to walk up the driveway towards the street. It was then I heard it: in my mind a voice said, "Push open the door and crouch down." It was a voice similar to the one I'd heard that night at Parkgate, and this time I recognised it much more easily. I moved towards the door again and, placing my hand against the rough surface, I gently pushed. I knew its limits this time, and whilst pushing it, I started to lower myself down, all the time looking through the opening. I could see there were wooden chairs in there which looked like they'd been thrown in. The damp heat hit me in my face as I got closer to the opening and there, in the corner of the shed to my right, I could make out his little face with tear-stained cheeks, his wide eyes staring straight at me. I could see he was trapped; the chairs were across him and it looked like they'd fallen on top of him, blocking his exit and holding him down. He was positioned exactly as I'd seen in my vision, and from that I knew how scared he must have been feeling.

I reached out my hand and tried to lift the chair in front of him, but I couldn't get enough of a grip. I asked him if he was OK and he just nodded – he never spoke at all.

I stood up quickly and shouted loudly, "He's here!" then barged my shoulder firmly against the door to somehow help me gain access. It moved enough to let me get a part way in, and as I did so, I started to lift off the wood that was piled high above him. I was aware of the sound of his mum's voice in the street, and so I shouted again, "He's here," not sure if

I'd been heard. I kept telling him that his mum was coming and at the same time was attempting to lift the pieces of furniture that were holding him in the corner. It seemed like minutes but was probably more like thirty seconds before I finally made my way in enough to lift the chair that was holding him against the wall. As I lifted it up, he pulled the arm behind him free, took a big breath and started to lean forward. I noticed that he wasn't bleeding, and he started to crawl slowly past me and towards the opened door. It was at this point I heard the sound of people running towards me – they were finally on their way – and his mum was crying his name. He crawled out of the shed at the exact moment his mum appeared behind me, and as she bent down to lift him up, he started to cry, and they just stood and sobbed together. She looked at me over his shoulder and, through her tears, just mouthed, "Thank you."

The police asked me what had happened and I explained how I had found him, although I said nothing about what had actually led me there. I made out that, like everyone else in the street, I was just checking possible places he could be and had happened to stumble across him. They concluded that he'd gone into the shed for some reason, had somehow disturbed the furniture, and it had collapsed onto him and blocked the exit. Apparently, and I still don't know why, he was unable to speak and therefore couldn't shout for help, leaving him not only trapped in the shed, but also trapped in his body too. I still shudder now thinking how petrified he must have felt.

So how did I know where to find him? What had happened within me to give me such a clear knowledge of his experience? I immediately went to my room to think it over and to understand the process behind my experience of what had just occurred. I knew that I had not been given the information by the Spirit World; not once did I feel the presence of someone who had died, nor did I see anyone who had guided me to him. It felt incredibly different to the time that I had stood up to demonstrate or to give a private sitting. Instead, I felt it was a direct connection to him. I recalled the images of him and of his feelings; it was like being in his head, in his body and in his feelings. I had glimpsed into his world in that moment. It was my intention to find him that had really begun the process of connection, my desire to understand his experience. Even now as I write this, I can still recall the sense of desperation I felt from him and I believe that it was being in my sensitive state that facilitated me to tap in to his feelings, feelings which eventually took me to him. Maybe what also helped was that he wanted to be found, and on that sensitive level I heard his 'call' and followed it. It was his need that pulled me to him; I just responded to that need.

CHAPTER 6

EXPERIENTIAL MEDIUMSHIP

By now I was attending the church in Stainforth regularly, as well as doing the occasional service or demonstration around Yorkshire too – it seemed that word had spread of a 'new kid on the block'. I was building confidence in my mediumship, and it started to feel more consistent and I seemed to be establishing a clear 'style' of working. Usually when I connected with the Spirit World there would be a constant stream of flowing information, sometimes almost too fast for me to catch up with: the voices would flow, the images would come and I would walk, or pace, as they did so. I didn't have time to think about what or how I was receiving, and sometimes nor did the recipient; they would be bombarded with information from their loved ones. People used to say I was like a 'Gatling gun'. I was often told to 'slow down' or 'remember to breathe' as I worked, but it seemed something I wasn't able to control or affect. Sometimes the information was incredibly specific, things that I could never have known about a person. There were occasions when I would see telephone numbers in mid-air; these numbers were later confirmed as belonging to the loved ones in Spirit. On occasion, I would hear the full names of people in the audience as a means of being able to identify who the communication was for.

However, in the early days I often wondered whether I was making it all up, whether mediumship was real or whether all those years of being alone in my bedroom had really just helped the emergence of a very fertile imagination. I would sometimes sit and question whether my imagination, and my need to be validated and liked in an environment that made me feel special and safe, was really behind this mediumship thing. There were certainly times when I would speak to recipients about things that were happening in their lives that were startlingly similar to things that I'd also experienced. When I was trying to explain to people about their mum or dad, I would sometimes see my own parents; and at other times when the people in the Spirit World were trying to describe where they lived or what they liked, they would show me images of where I'd been or I'd relive my own preferences; it was like recalling my own memories. Maybe I was just highly perceptive and sensitive to people and that was it, perhaps the Spirit World didn't exist at all? I was having a spiritual crisis!

I'd certainly noticed a change in myself after the air rifle incident; I was intently questioning what I was attracting into my life. This in turn made me examine what was happening within my mediumship. I'd already recognised that when I was in full flow it was like I'd almost 'stepped back' in my mind; I was still very much aware of the Spirit World, I wasn't in a trance of any kind, but a part of me was observing the information as I received it rather than being in it. It was like a version of Darren was watching another version of Darren receive the information. It didn't seem to interfere with the process and it was interesting to notice how I'd somehow 'withdrawn' my own conscious mind from the process. It gave me the opportunity to notice that as I received information I was able to assess how specific I thought it was. There were also times when the information I 'received' seemed so generic and vague that it seemed barely valuable, because so many people could have accepted it as also being true for them. It didn't stop me delivering the information, but it was through this evaluation I became clearer about what was good evidence and what wasn't. Of course, it was my perception of the evidence and, generally speaking, all the evidence we deliver as mediums is completely subjective, because it isn't about us.

I'd observed a pattern in the communicators I was attracting. It didn't matter where I demonstrated, occasionally I would get evidence from a grandmother in the Spirit World who had liked to bake. She presented wearing an apron, her hair was curly and her sleeves were rolled up. She was a kind woman, loved children and was the matriarch of the family; in my experience of her, she was always accompanied by the smell of cakes and bread, and she always drank out of a china cup and saucer. There was additional information which happened to be different from the other grandmothers; the names were different, the description of where they lived as well, along with other identifying information such as dates, places and certain memories. She didn't appear at every venue I worked, but whenever a grandmother came forward from the Spirit World she usually presented initially in the same way. Interestingly, on the occasions I watched other mediums demonstrate, they also mentioned a similar grandmother type: a kind woman who baked, was a matriarch and who loved children. Surely not ALL grandmothers are like this? I'm sure there must be grandmothers in the world who didn't like children, who never baked cakes and were as mean as hell! So, if that was the case, then why didn't I ever receive that type, and more to the point, why didn't the other mediums seem to either? Having had the experience of 'like attracts like' in my life, I was inspired to examine my mediumship through that lens of reflection.

I was blessed to know both my grandmothers and I loved them both dearly. They were very different from each other in pretty much all ways: Maud was tall and slim, whereas Vera was shorter and more cuddly. Vera was child-friendly and Maud wasn't. At Nanna Vera's house we would be guaranteed to be given unlimited homemade cakes and sweet pies, and at Gran Maud's we were only ever allowed one sweet from the jar under the coffee table – she never liked 'greedy children'. The fact that Maud was born on Halloween did nothing to enhance her grandmotherly image to me. Although she was a kind woman, straight speaking, she was definitely from a 'children should be seen and not heard' generation. Nanna Vera, however, loved to have her grandchildren to visit and had a cheerier disposition; she wore an apron, baked every Friday, and always drank out of a china cup and saucer, never a mug. Eureka! I got it! It finally occurred to me that the grandmother I was describing in other people's communications was fundamentally my own Nanna Vera. This was such a revelation to me, and it made me wonder whether this was also true for other mediums. It was certainly a plausible theory; after all, if we communicate to the Spirit World with our minds and our experiences of life, and we also attract what we give out, then it would make complete sense. What if a part of the initial communication is about us, and a part of it becomes more about the individuality of the communicator in Spirit as the contact progresses?

I'd never really examined the process of connecting with the Spirit World and blending with the communicators in detail. I would usually just send a prayer to them and say, "I'm ready," believing it was the intent alone that created the experience of mediumship. Then my mind would quieten and I'd start to see or hear something, and then we were off. This new insight made me examine the process more fully because it was important to know what was happening within me as I made that link.

What I concluded so far was that the information or people that were a part of my own life experience seemed to be used by the communicators in the Spirit World; they would somehow bring to the surface my own memories, because there were similarities to their own. It appeared the memories that came up within me were only those about situations, places, names or people with which I resonated positively. I'd noticed that this tended to happen in the early stages of the communication. After that initial 'introduction', the information became much more personal and specific to the communicator, and much less about my own experiences. It was at that point in the demonstration that I would also start to feel the presence of the person in Spirit much more.

I started to observe other mediums intently with this new understanding in mind. I wanted to assess for myself whether they were also giving this 'generalised' and non-specific information as a part of their communications. Interestingly, this seemed to be the case, and it wasn't just with grandmothers either! I would notice older mediums talking to older recipients about the war, something the mediums had also had direct experiences of. They would reminisce about tin baths in front of the fire, ration books and Anderson shelters, and the recipients would nod in agreement and then profess what wonderful evidence of survival they'd received, even though some of this information wasn't attached to a particular communicator. It appeared that the information was accurate, but not outstanding, because it was more about the medium's experience, rather than the individuality of the people who had passed away. I would also see mediums delivering names and sometimes saying before them, "Oh, this is my daughter's name, but can you understand the name..." It seemed that familiarity was somehow relevant in this type of mediumship. What I also observed is that some mediums would work in this way for the complete length of time they demonstrated, some started that way and then expanded into more detail and specifics, but every medium I saw, and have seen since, works with a combination of these two elements.

So, the problem with a medium working in this manner is that it has exposed them to criticism. The purpose of mental mediumship is to offer people evidence of life after death of the individual. It doesn't matter who communicates; the recipient should be able to identify the communicator, because the information, memories and details given are so incredibly specific to their loved one it could only be their loved one and no-one else. The other aspect to working this way is that the 'evidence' given by the medium wasn't strong enough to offer a therapeutic benefit to the recipient. The observer would assess the communication and the recipients' responses and assume it was accurate, but the truth was it was so generalised, it could have been accepted by most people. To the sceptic observing the same demonstration, they would not even consider they were witnessing the Spirit World communicating at all; to them this was a type of Forer effect in action beautifully.

If you do a search online for the Forer effect you can read more about it, but Wikipedia states the following:

> "The Barnum effect, also called the Forer effect, is a common psychological phenomenon whereby individuals give high accuracy ratings to descriptions of their personality that supposedly are tailored specifically to them but that are, in fact, vague and general enough to apply to a wide range of people."

The above explanation relates to how a character or personality of a person can be defined or described. What I witnessed in other medium's work, and also experienced within my own mediumship, is that the statements made weren't exclusively character or personality assessments, but also to the details of people's lives, including those in the Spirit World.

Through this evaluation, what became apparent is that this was more experiential mediumship than evidential mediumship and was due mainly to the influence of the medium's emotional state or experiences, rather than the Spirit communicators. It seemed that experiential mediumship was also influenced by both generation and culture. For example, the majority of grandmothers in my generation baked, were matriarchs and drank out of a china cup; ultimately, it was appropriate to that era. Grandmothers in modern day aren't so likely to conform to that stereotype anymore – they're more likely to be playing bingo on their iPads, getting tattoos done and taking part in extreme sports rather than baking cakes!

From what I had observed, as the link formed between the medium and the communicator, a part of the 'tuning in' process was about the communicator finding shared experiences or similarities and bringing those memories to the surface in the medium's mind. I felt that they did this as a way of both utilising the experiences of the medium to assist them giving information about themselves, and also somehow harnessing the medium's energy to help with the communication process. At this stage, it was mainly the mind of the medium in operation and the information they were in touch with wasn't particularly evidence of life after death – it was more evidence of the medium's life and experiences. It appeared that the medium had a couple of ways to go from this point: they could deliver the information, knowing it to be about the person in Spirit using their own memories to start the process, or they could see this information as purely their own mind and totally dismiss it, therefore disconnecting from the person in Spirit who is trying to build the connection. If they chose the former and the medium moved their awareness more fully onto the Spirit communicator, then the information would begin to become much more specific, in effect to become much more about the communicator and much less about the medium.

With experiential mediumship, as people evolve generationally then there should also be an evolution which takes place within that mediumship too. What that would mean in reality is that there may come a time when grandmothers baking cakes become such a rare thing that it can't be in the experience of the medium anymore and therefore can't be used as experiential evidence as a part of Spirit communication; it could only be evidential mediumship.

The more I explored mediumship, the more I recognised that the medium was the most important aspect of the process. The medium was the conduit for the information from the Spirit World and I recognised that the closer the communicator was to the medium, and the less the medium got involved – whether consciously or otherwise – the purer the communication was, meaning the evidence was more accurate and precise too. In the early days, anything related to mediumship and psychic work was fascinating to me. I read so many books about mediums, I'd listen to their lectures and I'd watch as many mediums as possible in order to understand my own mediumship. Now, armed with this new revelation that the medium was the most important part of the process, I became fascinated and I wanted to push myself further.

CHAPTER 7

EVIDENCE

What constitutes evidence of life after death? It's a huge question and one which, rightly so, is entirely individual. For some people, if a medium were to tell them something only they would know, this is enough. For others, it's the speaking of things that ARE known that bring about the healing. It's the personal, unique, sometimes quirky, factual pieces of information that a loved one will bring, which moves the sitter from grief into joy. It's the things only they would know, AND sometimes the things they have to check for accuracy, that open them to the healing. As mediums, all we have to 'sell' people so they accept the reality of the Spirit World is the individual evidence of it. Sure, people may come along to see you demonstrate because you're humorous, work quickly, give lots of messages or are new to the church, but the truth is, as a medium it's the quality of your work and the clarity of the evidence you deliver which will bring people back for a second visit.

One of the difficulties in people accepting the reality of the Spirit World is that sometimes mediums' communications are ambiguous, are open to the sitter's interpretation, or they give information which really can't be validated at all. Sometimes there are platitudes offered such a 'she loves you and is proud of you' or there are references to sentiment such as 'he loved the old times.' I've often heard comments such as 'he worked with his hands' which actually says nothing because unless you're a footballer or have no hands, pretty much everyone does! Are these statements comforting to hear? Undoubtedly. Do any of these statements offer proof of the continuation of life? Not at all. That isn't to say we should never say them; they do have a value, but only when they're also supported by clear, precise facts about the loved one in Spirit – information that can be validated. When you boil it down, it is evidence of life after death being based on facts and not just on feeling and sentiment alone.

As an example of what I mean, here's a 'reading' I have made up, using some of the statements I have heard mediums give along the way – how much of it is right for you?

The first thing I felt was that you have a great deal of unused capacity, which you have not yet tapped in to. One of your great strengths is that you're really disciplined and self-controlled on the outside, but you tend to worry a lot and sometimes feel insecure inside. It seems that sometimes you have a great need for other people to like and admire you.

You prefer a certain amount of change and variety, but you hate to be told what to do, and you get frustrated by restrictions and limitations. You're such an independent thinker, but you won't accept other people's opinions without satisfactory proof – you're strong-minded. You tend to be critical of yourself and when you can't sleep it's usually because you can't switch off your mind. At times, you have serious doubts as to whether you have made the right decision or done the right thing and you worry what people will think. At times you are extroverted, sociable, while at other times you are introverted, wary and reserved.

Generally, you are a cheerful and friendly person, but I could see there has been a time in the past when you were very upset. You still think about that moment sometimes and you haven't fully got over it; it was a really difficult time for you. I feel that your relationship with your parents was challenging sometimes – one of them was emotionally distant – but you tried your best to make the relationship work.

I got the feeling that at some point you've been thinking about writing a book and someone around you is researching family history. I also saw that you've wanted to clear out some cupboards and drawers but haven't got around to it yet!

I felt the initial 'J' was really significant to you? There was also an older lady in Spirit who passed with an illness who's watching over you, and an older man between his seventies and eighties who worked with his hands. They were both proud of you said you were doing really well!

I suspect that a fair bit of the reading above would apply to you? This is because the majority of the statements above are what psychologists would call 'Barnum statements', or the Forer effect, as mentioned in the previous chapter. These statements sound very specific and factual, but in truth they would apply to a large proportion of the population. As you can see, they're ambiguous, sometimes conflicting, vague, often show you favourably and you actually apply your own meaning to the reading, which in many cases determines its success.

As a developing medium I was always very sceptical when watching this form of 'platitude mediumship.' It made no sense to me that recipients were making the 'evidence' fit them somehow. Or they were accepting platitudes as communication from their loved one, and then saying what lovely evidence they had even though none was presented. They would sometimes even accept information from the medium that was plainly incorrect but took it anyway and claimed that THEY had made a mistake. I would always wonder why the Spirit World would give information that couldn't be validated? Surely in a demonstration where the intent was to offer proof of life after 'death', why would they give information which couldn't be validated? Maybe, then, the issue is about the intent of the medium or their own understanding of what constitutes evidence? What was clear during these kinds of demonstrations was there was evidence of the medium's awareness to some degree being presented, but not evidence of the Spirit World's existence.

From my very first visit to a spiritualist church when I was an observer, I always felt clear about which information was vague or wishy-washy, and what was clear and precise. I think this was helped by my various occupations, some of which were detail-orientated; you can't be wishy-washy whilst wiring a house a with a 240-volt power supply or be ambiguous in the recording of patients' information in the optometrists where I had also worked. It was this mentality of having to 'get it right' combined with a clear idea on what is evidence of life after death, which ultimately moved my mediumship into communicating more precise information. On reflection, I also recognise that as a young boy, I was very much filled with feelings of inadequacy which motivated me into reaching out to 'be more' to eradicate my feelings of shame. Given what I now understand, the progression towards 'more' seemed to be reflected in the evidence too.

What has also become increasingly clear with time is that our mediumship is a combination of our life experiences and our expectations. Experiential mediumship covers a part of our awareness where we bring this aspect to the mix just by being present. We must cultivate and constantly review our expectations. Now I'm not talking about the expectation that we have a set list of evidence that we must tick off in robotic style during every communication; nor where we make demands of the communicators and expect them to conform to our pre-conceptions in order to please us. No, I'm speaking of a type of expectation where we lovingly, and strongly, know that whatever information the communicators wish to deliver is available to us and will come if we don't interfere with the process.

The greatest mediums never approached the Spirit World with a half-hearted 'I really hope I get something' attitude. They went to it knowing the Other World's desire was to demonstrate the reality of their presence, and the medium knew that ALL information to support the communicator's presence was available to them within their mediumship. If a communicator wanted to give their name, it was received by the medium, so too their address, their hobbies, their work

– in fact, every piece of information about their own life was available and the medium just had to be in alignment with them to receive it.

Below are examples of the types of information we should be looking for in mediumship, both as a recipient and as a medium:

Names/nicknames	Significant music/songs
Age at time of passing	Hobbies/interests
Physical description	Memories of events/ experiences
Scars/tattoos/disability	Work/hobbies
Relationship to recipient	Emotional life
How they 'died'	How they preferred to dress
Associated family i.e. children	Illnesses and how it affected them
Significant dates	Personality
Address including type of house, bungalow, etc.	Likes/dislikes
Favourite foods/drinks	'Codes' between communicator and recipient

Being clear about what evidence is and isn't was so important because I recognised there was a clear link between my INTENT and the CONTENT in my work. My intent was always that the Spirit World would deliver clear, precise information that offered people proof of an afterlife, and the content of the communication was always supportive of that. Sometimes there would be a vast stream of information, names, dates, places, all in quick succession, and at other times there were only a couple of pieces of information. I remember the shortest private reading I ever gave only contained two pieces of information; I knew the sitter's mum had passed, and in my mind's eye I saw an orange in a lady's hand. Now, in all the years of doing mediumship prior to this, I knew better than to doubt their intelligence, but REALLY? How could I say to a woman, "Your mum is here and she's holding an orange"? Before I even said it, it sounded like nonsense, but in the absence of receiving anything else, and with the sitter looking at me expectantly, I took the risk. I took a breath and hoped to God that something else would come along after offering the orange that was coherent, clear and evidential.

"Your mum is here and she's holding an orange." There was a gasp and her eyes widened as she put her hand to her mouth and burst into tears. I remember little else of the sitting other than she later explained to me that she and her mum had a pact before death that if there was an afterlife, the one who survived would see a medium, and the 'code word' was 'orange' to prove they were fine in the afterlife. It was that particular sitting which helped me to reassess what evidence looked like and what was valid evidential content.

I think it's important to recognise that there is a very clear distinction between evidence of life after death, and proof of it. Our job as mediums is to deliver evidence, to give the information we receive and work at presenting the information as specifically as we can. Even when we do so, and WE are satisfied with it, to others it may still not be proof of an afterlife because it didn't meet the sitter's expectations. What constitutes proof of an afterlife is different for everyone. Some people require little, as with the lady for whom the evidence of an orange was enough, yet some people require much more. As a result of that experience, I gained a deeper trust in the evidence I received and, more importantly, I realised that I need not judge it nor assess whether it was 'enough' by MY standards. Evidence takes place in the experience of the medium, but only proof can take place in the mind of the recipient.

§

If I were to choose which type of evidence was the most impactful, I would have to say without question, the personality. Yes, of course, names, addresses, descriptions, and personal codes and so on are vital from a factual perspective, but it's in the reaching for a communicator's personality that also has a greater benefit to everyone in the process. Why? Because it's all about connection.

> The personality can be defined as being made up of three parts:
> 1. The communicator's consistent thoughts.
> 2. The communicator's consistent feelings.
> 3. The communicator's consistent behaviours.

When we look at the people in our lives – our friends and family – what are the components that positively connect us? Usually we share similar thoughts, feelings and behaviours.

Generally speaking, it's why nuns hang around nuns and bikers hang around bikers! We love those qualities and aspects in others that resemble our own, and we tend to shy away from people whose don't. So, when we describe a communicator in the Spirit World, that process also goes on. We resonate positively towards people who have a similar vibe to us and we also feel it when they don't, and it is through being available to the communicator in this process that we can emotionally connect with them. We are in a privileged position as mediums to have access to their thoughts, feelings and behaviours as part of an evidential communication, and it's vital we somehow integrate that into our evidence along with the factual elements. A well-known saying is, "You will forget what a person said, you will forget what a person did, but you will NEVER forget how a person made you feel."

The truth is, if we ONLY give factual information, some of this can be forgotten by the recipient and therefore can't be validated – for example, I wouldn't remember now the colour of my grandad's eyes if you told me. If, however, you were to ask me to describe my grandad's personality and how I felt in his presence, I will always remember that.

The other process that occurs, which is not only helpful in achieving greater evidence but also in the recipient having a therapeutic experience of mediumship, all stems from identifying the personality. Once we reach into the personality of the Spirit person, we have access to their emotions and how they felt; this moves us into their mind and how they thought. This in turn leads us to accessing the experiences they had in life and how they behaved, which in turn opens us up to more evidence. This, combined with the description of their personality, has the potential to move the recipient towards a place of healing.

It's true that the more specific the evidence we reach for in our mediumship, the more we think there is greater 'risk' of us getting it wrong. We sometimes, and mostly unconsciously, keep the evidence 'small' to mitigate the chance of that happening. For example, we know we can deliver so much clear information without giving a full name and so there is an unconscious resistance to moving towards receiving that type of evidence. We know that if we end the communication by saying, "...and his name is Peter Morrison," we are putting our necks on the chopping block and taking a huge risk, thereby potentially losing the trust of the audience or of our sitters. In essence we stay in our comfort zones and we don't extend a curiosity to the Spirit World to expand on what we receive from them. So, the key to us receiving, and more importantly delivering, that information is:

1. Being clear about what constitutes evidence of life after death and what doesn't.
2. Knowing that all information is available.
3. Being curious about our communicators.
4. Being vulnerable and yet trusting enough to voice everything we experience.

CHAPTER 8

BOUNDARIES

A boundary is a space that defines the area in which you are willing to be present. Boundaries can be mental, physical, emotional, spiritual and energetic; time is also a boundary. Boundaries are the constructs that actually keep us safe. There is no greater situation where it's vital to our well-being to have them than when we are working with people in need.

I was twenty-one, the 'new kid/medium on the block', and three years in, I was working all hours, every week and every weekend, because somewhere along the line it was said to me that I must always use the gifts God had given me or I would lose them. They were, after all, given to be used for others at ALL times in ALL places; saying no wasn't an option. By saying no, I was told many times that I would upset God and everyone else in the process. The phone never stopped ringing and I never stopped answering it; people turned up for sittings unannounced and I did them. People asked me to travel to places I'd never even heard of and I did, regardless of what I may have preferred to do on my birthday, on Mother's Day or any other day that mattered to me. All this I did, whilst holding down my apprenticeship, working full time and attending college twelve hours per week. In effect, I became a doormat.

When you have an ability, a gift or a 'thing' AND you are brought up well, you are taught you must share what you have with others less fortunate than yourself. We are told as children that sharing our sweets would mean that we're a 'good person' and doing so would please our parents. The people in church reinforced that message with statements such as 'it's a gift from God, you should help everyone you can with it' and comments such as 'you shouldn't charge, it was given to you freely'. In effect, we're taught that in order to be loved and accepted, we have to give something of ourselves away, regardless of whether that makes us happy or not. When you've learned to people-please, in a place where pleasing is revered, you're also willing to give up not only what you have but also who and what you are.

I was asked to take a service at a local church and, as usual, I accepted. A couple of weeks later I found myself on platform, exhausted, but faking the feeling of being pleased to be there. At the beginning of the service I was acutely conscious of a lady in the audience who appeared very troubled; she looked unkempt and there was a heaviness about her that seemed not only to weigh her down but also those nearby. For the purposes of maintaining her anonymity I will call her Lorraine. She took a card at the end of the service and said she would contact me for a sitting. As I touched her hand, my awareness told me clearly not to see her. I had no explanation as to why not, just a strong desire to say no, not to offer her an appointment. My instinct was screaming no, and yet the people-pleasing voice in my head told my instinct to shut its mouth! First thing on Monday morning the phone rang and a slow, drawn-out voice began to speak without taking a breath. On hearing her voice, the knot in my stomach formed again, and one minute later her name was written in my diary for an appointment; I couldn't say no, as she might be upset and it wasn't 'spiritual'. A week later, and twenty minutes into the sitting, it became clear that this lady had suffered years of abuse through various relationships and as a result had developed serious mental health problems. She was desperate to know when she would be better and if she would find peace. I spent time chatting after the sitting, giving her my time – time I couldn't really afford to spare but felt I 'should'. I left her house more tired than when I'd started and sent up a prayer for her as I walked away.

A few days later she called, this time saying she was being haunted by spirits and demanded that I should go over to her house and get rid of whatever was disturbing her. Knowing that there wasn't an issue with the spirit people, I declined, believing that the issue was more about her mental health. Finally, after calming her down and chatting with her, she asked me if I could send her a photograph of me as she felt very calmed whenever we spoke or when she thought of me. She said the photo would 'make the pain go away'. I made a joke about it not being the best cure for feeling depressed and changed the subject. During our conversation I'd mentioned to her that my mum hadn't been well at the time and how I needed to spend more time with her. Over the next few days

I'd become more aware of 'Lorraine' around the town close to my home, to the point where it seemed wherever I went she was there. She would stare at me through shop windows or send her daughter over to speak to me.

One particular day not long after I received a call from my nanna, asking me when I would visit her as arranged that day. I told Nanna I was going to be longer than usual, as I'd agreed to squeeze in a sitting before setting out. She said, "It's just that Lorraine is here and she turned up with some flowers for your mum and she said she won't leave until she sees you."

At this point alarm bells rang, such that I couldn't ignore them, but it was too late. I had given Lorraine, and others, open access into my life. By not being clear on what was acceptable to me, I had also given her and others permission to behave exactly as they wished.

Actually, we teach people how to treat us. If we don't make the choices necessary to live the lives we desire, then we give permission to the people in our life to choose our experiences for us. In effect, we live by default. When we try to enforce those boundaries with people without explaining to them WHY we need to do so, they get angry. Because I knew this, and because I also knew Lorraine was mentally ill, I chose not to explain to her my reasons for stepping back, and instead I just cut her off and ceased to respond to her calls. After a few months, I had heard no more and thought it had been dealt with... and this proved to be the case with Lorraine, but I still hadn't asserted my boundaries clearly enough. Whilst I was clearer about what not to disclose to others, I still wasn't clear about how to handle saying no to people, and I made no changes to when or how I worked. In fact, the only changes I did make were to not visit people's houses to give sittings. It wasn't really the whole answer and I knew it. You see, we can do our best to cheat ourselves, but we can't cheat life or the Universe; it remembers and brings to us what we need to learn.

Several years later, and still not honouring myself or my needs, I was asked to take a charitable demonstration in Sheffield. It was at the end of a full week of demonstrations and I'd agreed to share the demonstration with a friend to raise money for the Make a Wish Foundation. I'd had a phone call from a chap named Peter who wanted to make a £200 donation to the funds. I was very grateful and invited him to a local demonstration in Sheffield so that I could meet and thank him in person. Before the actual demonstration, I'd had quite a few phone calls from him, all very pleasant and undemanding – and yet the alarm bells I'd previously 'heard' started tinkling again.

In my mind, that evening produced one of the poorest demonstrations I've ever given. Whatever the reason, I just didn't seem to be able to 'connect', either to the audience or to the Spirit World; it was hard work! As I stood on the platform looking into the audience of two hundred people, I saw a man slightly shorter than myself with a beard, moustache and glasses. I'd noticed him because he seemed transfixed; everywhere I walked, his eyes followed. There was something about him that made me feel very uncomfortable and yet at that time I didn't know why. The end of the demonstration couldn't come soon enough and when it did, I invited Peter to the speakers' room to thank him for the money he'd donated. It turned out he was the bearded bespectacled audience member I'd observed from the platform. He was gushing about how wonderful the demonstration was, how accurate, how professional, to the point where I again felt incredibly uncomfortable, and not just because I didn't feel I'd done justice to the evening of mediumship – there was something about his enthusiasm that alarmed me. Our cups of tea arrived shortly afterwards and, in my eagerness to rush away, I dropped some of the biscuit I was eating into my lap. No sooner had it landed than Peter leaned over, picked up the biscuit and ate it! Shocked was not the word. I jumped off the chair and asked him what he thought he was doing; at this point the secretary of the event came into the room. The situation calmed and I left, fuming. His behaviour was a step too far and I was angry at him for crossing a line. "How dare he?" A stranger, behaving so inappropriately and not honouring my personal space. "Who did he think he was that he could do that to me?!"

The journey home was full of these questions and more frustration. Peter's phone calls continued, he turned up at almost every demonstration I did and I became increasingly anxious about the intrusion, and because I did not want to offend him or hurt his feelings, I still didn't say so. In my mind, I felt I was public property and I had no right to say no; this was a gift, and I must always use it and be 'nice' to people. That's what people-pleasers do, isn't it? It was certainly how I'd always operated and it didn't seem to do me any harm, or so I thought.

The final straw came when I arrived at Ashby Spiritualist Church in Scunthorpe to take a Saturday demonstration. I left the speakers' room and headed to the platform to start the demonstration. I turned, sat down, looked up and the first person I saw was him, smiling as if nothing had happened. The rush of emotions sent me off balance for a moment. I was still reeling from a conversation I'd had with him that week when he wished me luck for my upcoming tonsillectomy. I hadn't even mentioned to him that I was having the operation and still to this day I have no idea how he knew. The feelings were not at all pleasant: my mouth went dry, my heart started racing and my head started to spin. At any moment I was going to die, I felt sure of it. The room began to swim and the contents of my stomach seemed to be lurching for an exit. There was no way I could demonstrate. What was happening to me? I stood up to speak, and then apologised and sat down – I couldn't do it. I couldn't even pretend I was OK; apparently the colour drained from my face. I left the church quickly – upset, frightened, panicky and most of all angry. For the second time, "How dare he?"

The diagnosis for my episode at Scunthorpe was social phobia and panic disorder. It certainly explained why I avoided going out anywhere unless it was dark and there were no people around. It explained why I'd cancelled all of my work, and it also explained the need to see a psychotherapist for eighteen months so I could leave the house more easily and eventually get back to living my life. It was during one of the sessions with the therapist that the answer hit me like a bucket of cold water to the face. This issue wasn't really about anyone else but me; Peter was only the person who came into my life to bring the blessing to me. What had I done to create the situation I had found myself in? The truth was, I had given Peter complete permission to access my life because of my refusal to be clear about the need to honour my space and to say no when his attention became uncomfortable. I had people-pleased my way into this situation and honoured someone else's needs above and beyond my own. He needed a friend, and for a while I felt it would be wrong to refuse that. He needed someone to talk to, and I answered the phone because of my mistaken belief that I should be accessible and offer help to everyone at all times. He also needed to see me work because on some level it helped him – who was I to not allow that? Now I had finally seen it, neither Peter nor Lorraine were the only two people this belief applied to. In pretty much all of my connections to people I had conformed to the role of 'public property'. Coupled with my need to people-please, the belief that I should never say no AND the thought that I would upset Spirit or God in the process if I did, this sent me both temporarily crazy and also led me to this revelation in a psychotherapist's office. I was in this situation because I hadn't defined the space in which I was willing to be present and I had also not been brave enough to voice it. I gave so much of myself away and then became angry when people didn't treat me as I wanted to be treated.

When you're in a role that involves meeting the needs of others, there is a requirement for boundaries. Before you can truly fulfil that role in a way that doesn't deplete you, there is a need to be clear on whom you are, your capabilities, your limitations and your desires. There is a need to be clear on these things because people with unfulfilled needs aren't able to *be* these things for themselves. Forgetting our strength, being fearful, and not trusting life and its process all motivate people to reach out to someone they feel could help to remind them of these things. Lorraine and now Peter were only acting upon their need to be 'heard' and their right to be understood by someone who they felt held an answer to their unfilled needs. The 'message' I had sent out was that I'm always available, always here, always helpful, always your friend. They were only guilty of responding to the message I put out; I felt that I was guilty of so much more.

The Universe constantly offers us the opportunity to re-evaluate our choices and to make better ones, but it can only ever provide the very same value we place on ourselves. If, as I did, you give yourself away to everyone and everything, life will bring to you people and situations who will support you in losing who and what you are. If you also play the 'Why me?' victim role, you will also attract more of the same experiences because the Universe interprets your request as 'give me more information', and so it does. I had thought and behaved my way into this situation, and now that I had this new-found awareness, I had to make better choices about what I wanted to experience and then behave my way towards experiencing them. We get signs from the Universe, always. These signs are the wisest way the Universe can communicate with us, but we often dismiss them out of hand because of our humanness and need to be right. I had the *thought* that I shouldn't have seen Lorraine, but I chose to ignore it. Because I refused to listen to the thought, I then developed an *emotion* about seeing her. Again, I chose to ignore the feeling, and so I then developed a *physical* response to the situation which in turn led to a physical effect involving my family. It was exactly the same with Peter – my refusal to 'take the hint' eventually left me with crazy thoughts, confused emotions and eventually very physical panic attacks. Denial by its very nature creates a density within our energy field which is directly proportionate to the level of resistance we have to that wisdom. The more we resist or ignore these signs, the more pain we experience – first in our thoughts, then our emotions and eventually in our physical being. Putting other people's needs first was very easy for me – I'd been doing it for years. However, honouring my own needs proved to be more of a challenge.

So, what IS our role and responsibility as mediums? Should we say no, and will we offend or upset God if we do? I'm sure that depending on the medium or person, you'll get a different response, and there is no right or wrong, only what's appropriate to each individual. Of course, everyone's experience and perception of God is unique, but the idea that God behaves as humans do doesn't sit well with me. I don't accept that He or She is making a judgement on our behaviours and issuing a punishment if we displease them. I don't really believe that the mediumistic ability is a 'gift', anyway; I think as we are all Spirit, the ability to communicate with those in the Spiritual Realms is inherent with everyone to some degree – the 'gift' is how we utilise it. There seemed to be a way of thinking within spiritualism that 'suffering' and 'sacrificing' ourselves is OK, and unfortunately in some ways it's applauded. I listen to my instinct much more now than ever; I certainly have no desire to suffer for my work, and I don't believe God would expect us to either, as it would benefit no-one. *A Course in Miracles* teaches that when we sacrifice ourselves for others we make the people we're helping wrong because we're letting them harm us, and they don't know they're doing it. So, giving to others to our own detriment is actually unkind to all parties!

CHAPTER 9

DEVELOPMENT

"How do I develop my gift?", "Can you train people to be mediums or healers?", "I'm not religious, do I have to believe in God to be a medium?" and "How long will it take and how much will it cost?" These are the most common questions I've been asked in relation to the development of mediumship. I always find it interesting, if a little disheartening, to hear that in the unfolding of their soul and its purpose, people need a time frame and a price before they're willing to 'invest'. It is no longer a surprise that students also want some form of guarantee. After they've delivered their first communication in the development group, I will hear questions such as, "So after six weeks I'll be a medium?" or "When will I be able to give my first demonstration?" As my nanna would say, "Don't run before you can walk," and this is never truer than in the area of mediumistic and psychic unfoldment.

Do you ever remember as a child seeing a flower in bud and wondering what is inside the bud? Do you recall questioning how and why the petals are so tightly bound and wondering whether, if you're really careful, you could open it up? I do – I remember sitting in my grandad's garden, surrounded by roses, and seeing the most beautiful pink flower not yet open, and I wondered what it would smell like. So I picked it and I sat with it patiently and very gently, one by one, peeling every petal, trying my best to not tear any of them, motivated by the 'prize' of seeing and smelling the contents. Of course, it was an impossible task. Every petal had torn under the pressure because it was so delicate. As much as I tried to tease, cajole and squeeze the bud, the flower eventually fell apart, losing the scent and the essence of a beautiful thing. The truth is, the flower wasn't READY to open and the conditions weren't in place for that to happen at that time. Our spiritual and mediumistic unfoldment is exactly the same.

The majority of mediums' and healers' first experiences of the Spirit World – or, indeed, their abilities – are usually preceded by some highly emotional and sometimes traumatic event that somehow forces a change in the perception of their reality. For me it was illness, the loneliness of my childhood, and the intense focus on my sexuality and my emotional world at a very young age. For others it is bereavement, abuse or a near-death experience. Somehow this shift in awareness or reality, the suffering that seems to accompany it, as well as the huge focus on the emotional self, seems to accelerate an increasing sensitivity and compassion for others, but it is also pivotal in revealing our spiritual gifts and talents. In effect, this process spiritualises us, it reminds us that we are spiritual beings. Interestingly, this can also be true for people whose 'gifts of the Spirit' are expressed via singing, art, medicine or, indeed, any vocation that presents as a calling. That call is the soul waking up to its purpose.

In the modern day, our spiritual gifts are not exclusive to those believers in a faith or religion. There are many stories from around the world of people having supernatural experiences without having even heard the name of Jesus or Buddha, and so therefore we must explore and examine why. Noticeably, spirituality and religion are increasingly seen as being opposite and yet the 'spiritual gifts' continue to manifest themselves. The 'gifts of the Spirit' is the name given specifically within Christianity as endowments given by the Holy Spirit. These were supernatural gifts which individual Christians need (or needed, in the days of the Apostles) to fulfil the mission of the church. They are described in full in the New Testament and are related to both seemingly natural and miraculous abilities, empowered by the Holy Spirit. In effect they are gifts from God. Gifts such as clairvoyance, prophecy, healing, speaking in tongues, discerning of the Spirits and many others besides have parallels to our current experience of spiritualism, where the same experiences are given different names.

If we examine how common psychic experiences are, there are countless stories available to read online of people around the world experiencing spectacular things. There are stories of housewives and homemakers miraculously healing people without having had any religious experience, businessmen and women refusing to get on a plane because of a 'hunch' and then the plane crashing. Many of the bereaved of all faiths and cultures around the world regularly witness and have conversations with their deceased loved ones. So why does this happen outside the arena of religion, and what does it tell us about our own spiritual selves and our unfoldment? It also encourages us to ask whether mediumship and healing mediumship truly are gifts, as some practitioners would lead us to believe, or whether it is a special faculty bestowed only on the worthy by the divine, or those who are especially advanced in their spiritual evolution. Alternatively, consider that we are ALL of divine origin, and therefore we already come 'pre-installed' with the ability to connect to our spiritual home?

Did you choose these gifts or did they choose you? Did your awareness of the Spirit World find you, reveal itself and leave you with no alternative? Did it shake you up, wake you up and turn your life around? Or did you make a clear and conscious decision to explore your gifts in the same way you'd learn to play an instrument and fit it around your lifestyle and commitments without it really affecting you too much? When we're aligned with our soul's purpose, we really don't have a choice. When it's who we really are, and why we're here, there simply isn't an alternative. Of course, we can say we have choices and convince ourselves that we can abandon Spirit's purpose at any moment without consequences, but the absolute truth is that when it is in our soul's 'DNA' to do it, we don't have a choice.

There have been several occasions when I've put my mediumship 'on hold'. There were times when I've stopped demonstrating, stopped giving sittings, I wouldn't speak about it and in many other ways turned my back on it. Sometimes it has been from a need to rest, sometimes out of disappointment in spiritualism, sometimes because the experience didn't meet my own expectations and sometimes it's been because I've wanted to prove to myself that I could say no and not suffer any consequences. Whatever the reason for the breaks, they afforded me the opportunity to re-evaluate the work itself, my attachment to it, my reasons for doing it, and always I've come through those explorations with a renewed understanding of my relationship to the Spirit World. Without exception, regardless of my reasons for stepping back, I have always returned to it because NOT doing so was much more painful.

So, from a mediumship perspective, CAN we learn it? Mediumship, as mentioned, isn't limited to being a religious experience. As I am sure many of you are aware, its function does not depend upon mediums being always spiritually minded or, in some cases, just because they are nice people! As a teacher of mediumship, I can help you to increase your powers of perception, show you how to listen to the stillness within, and give you methods and exercises to access your sensitivity, but there are no guarantees that this will make you a medium or a healer. The decision as to whether you have the potential to be a medium I believe lies within your soul, not within your mind, your desire or how much money you throw at the subject.

Before we look in more detail about the 'how' of mediumship, I think it's more important to look at the 'why' people want to develop their awareness. The question I usually ask a potential student is, "Why do you want to be a medium?" The most common answer by far is, "I want to help people," which on the face of it is a noble and kind thing to offer, but I believe that statement actually originates in their ego. It is their desire to make well, their needing to feel a part of something bigger or their wanting to ease suffering that is really behind that statement. By saying that you want to help someone, often you're forming an opinion and sometimes making a judgement about what kind of help people need, often without even asking. We all know that our opinions and judgements can sometimes be wrong. As I've said previously, the soul and its power seeks to express itself, to be the demonstration of itself in the world. When your mind and personality are in alignment with your soul's desire, then help comes, regardless of your ego's needs. The only authentic answer to the question of why anyone would want to become a medium is, "I want to be of service to the Spirit and work with them in co-operation."

What is clear to me from my own experience is that when we start to explore ourselves spiritually, we will change. The power that we tap in to is transformative, that is to say, it encourages and supports growth on all levels of our life and our being, and it often means that parts of ourselves that require healing will come to the surface. Unfoldment can, as a result, be challenging for us, and sometimes for those around us too as they witness the effects. For those of you who have already begun this exploration, think of who and how you were before you began this, and then look at who you've become now. The change is tangible, isn't it? It's life-long and ongoing; we never get to the finish line, as there's always something more to explore.

Having been a medium since 1992 and having taught students in mediumship for the last sixteen years, I have noticed several changes. The most noticeable difference between mediumistic development now and that of the times of the great demonstrators of mediumship (Estelle Roberts, Alec Harris, Helen Hughes, etc. between the 1940s and 1980s), seems be two things: commitment and trust. If you go into any mediumship development circle, you're guaranteed to hear the phrase 'Trust in the Spirit World', and the sentiment behind that is we should drop our defences and be guided by the Spirit World. I think it's vital that we're very clear on the differences between 'trusting' and 'putting our trust in' something. Trust is often presented in a way that implies it's one thing, but when we use language in relation to our spiritual experiences, every word we say has power and therefore the outcome will be very different. Do you trust the Spirit World or do you put your trust in them?

When we say we trust Spirit, we are accepting their assistance. We're surrendering the need to be right, to be in control or to have to know everything. We're also placing our minds and our hearts into a state of allowing, accepting that we're always being guided by the intelligence of the Spirit World and knowing that they love us unconditionally; we then know that we can't ever fail in their eyes.

Whenever we say we are putting our trust *in* something, we're saying that we are expecting a need to be met, or a certain practice or framework to be adhered to, and we then start becoming attached to a pre-conceived outcome. We'll put pressure on ourselves to achieve a certain result which, if not met, can leave us beating ourselves up, blaming others (including Spirit sometimes) for our perceived failings, thereby creating self-sabotaging thoughts which are counter-productive to our intuition. When we put our trust in something, we're also on some level holding on to a need for validation or approval which also makes us fearful. This, in turn, can mistakenly lead us to believe that we'll suffer in some way for getting it wrong. So, I ask again, do you trust the Spirit World or do you put your trust in them?

In the days of great mediums such as Gordon Higginson, Albert Best and Estelle Roberts, they had learned to sit for the Spirit World regularly and without expectation, just to be in the presence of Spirit for the sake of it; they were committed to it. Their teachers understood the importance of the students taking time to blend with the Spirit World, to be clear in their understanding of the process first before they were even allowed to deliver communications. More importantly, it was consistently impressed upon them to just allow the influence of the Spirit. They were encouraged to accept the Spirit World's intelligence, to trust that it knew more than they did and to accept that the Spirit World knew what information they needed to know and would offer it to them when they were ready. In essence, the students moved at the pace of the Spirit World without interference; they trusted the Spirit and the process. That isn't to say that they didn't also have questions and I'm sure they asked exactly the same ones that today's students ask. I can imagine there was just as much impatience, frustration and doubting in themselves as there is with the students of today. However, I believe the difference back then was that they were invited to take those questions, frustrations and crises of confidences to the Spirit and ask for help there, rather than looking to their teacher to answer them, reassure them or validate them through their connection with the Spirit World.

In my opinion and experience, we've been encouraged to listen to the external voices too much and trust in them, rather than listening to the voice within us, leading us to just know from our own experience. I wonder whether this has partly contributed towards the decline in the quality of mediumship? It makes sense that if we push so hard for the result we want to achieve and make demands that the Spirit World conforms to our expectations, then we may unwittingly distort the link with them. This will, of course, negatively affect the accuracy of the communication. Over the years, so much of a student's focus seems to have been reduced by their tutors to the students finding certain specific pieces of information from their communicators in Spirit. Students are told they must ask the Spirit World questions to get better evidence. They are encouraged to ask things such as, "Can you give me your name?" or "How did you die?" We can now even go on courses to learn how to employ techniques to assist us in receiving certain identifying pieces of information such as age, physical descriptions, etc. The communicators seem to have to jump through a long list of questions so they can identify themselves, before we even comprehend what they want to communicate.

Now, of course, you're only really a medium if the information you deliver can be validated as proof and accepted by the recipient that their loved ones are indeed communicating from the Spirit World. It's therefore vital that we strive to receive more clear, precise and accurate information from them, but why don't we just let them get on with it and do all we can as the medium to not interfere in that process? The mother in Spirit knows what she can say to her son to free him from his grief. A daughter knows the 'code word' her mother told her to use prove an afterlife. The intelligence of the Spirit World goes far beyond our own, so why then do we put so much faith and trust in our methods rather than trusting theirs?

With this in mind, if you choose to explore your abilities further, then choose your teachers wisely. I believe the role of the teacher is about helping you to find the way that feels right, that will support you and encourage you not to be influenced by other people's experiences but to learn from your own. The best teachers will constantly remind and encourage you to be guided by the Spirit World and listen to the many different ways they will communicate with you. The author William Arthur Ward states that, "The mediocre teacher tells. The good teacher explains. The superior teacher demonstrates. The great teacher inspires."

Does your teacher tell, explain, demonstrate or inspire you? A wonderful way to examine whether a teacher is right for you is to watch them work and pay attention to how you feel in their presence. The language of the Spirit is always inspiring – in fact, the word inspiration contains the word Spirit within it, so when your intuition speaks, that's exactly what's happening: you're in tuition. You are learning something through that connection to your own soul, which is the wisest part of who you are. Are you listening to it? But, more importantly, are you feeling what you're hearing? Does your instinct shout, "Yes!" in response, or does it whisper, "No – that just doesn't feel right"? Because, as your level of understanding, experience and unfoldment grows, so will the range of phenomena and evidence that your mediumship contains and exhibits too. The best teacher you will ever have is the one within you; allow it to guide you in your understanding, regardless of whom you sit with.

As teachers, we are in a privileged and responsible position regarding our students' development. We are required to give answers to their questions; some can be wild and wacky, and others are grounded in common sense, coming from a desire to really understand their experience. We are afforded trust by the students, and we are expected to reassure and help them understand what they're going through. It's our job to clear up misunderstandings and misconceptions about the Spirit World and how we interact with it, as well as helping the students to recognise the impact and effect their awareness can have on them as the medium. If this part of our role is not being undertaken responsibly, we can actually create and increase fear in the student. Sadly, over the years I have heard horror stories; some students have been told utter nonsense more fitting for a Hollywood blockbuster than in a development group for potential mediums! Stories such as how you must protect yourselves from the 'bad spirits' that will enter you and possess you; others have been told that they should never eat meat because it will pollute the body and the Spirits won't work with you; even that you must have your mercury fillings removed or it will stop you communicating with the Spirit World at all!

I remember in the early days of my development, being so 'porous', I would literally take in and believe everything I was told without even questioning it. It had been suggested to me that healing mediumship might be a good thing to explore, and I did have a natural pull towards this discipline, so I signed up for the course. Part of the training was that I had to attend the healing service at the same church where I had learned about the mechanics of healing, as well as the administrative and legal aspects such as accurate record-keeping and healing in relation to people with cancer or AIDS. I would also, with supervision by the healing leader, deliver hands on healing to any patients who came in. This particular Tuesday I was feeling slightly frazzled after having had a chaotic morning and arrived at the healing class some minutes before it began. That day I'd missed breakfast, so I was quickly eating a packet of crisps as I was hungry. The healing leader took one look at me with my crisps in hand and in front of everyone shouted, "The Spirit World won't work with you on a full stomach!" I was absolutely shocked! Firstly, by the unprofessionalism of the leader to berate me in such a public way, but also without explanation of why the Spirit World would step away if I'd recently eaten. My rational mind was saying that surely if I was hungry, I would be constantly focussing on my body's needs and that would take my focus away from the connection with Spirit, and that wasn't a good thing? The student in me believed what I was told by the teacher, and so, for the next few weeks, I didn't eat before I attended the two-hour healing service which started at 11am. There were many times I was hungry and times I felt weak because of it, times when I had to sit down because I felt faint, and all because the teacher said I should be 'empty' to work as a healer. In hindsight, how foolish!

What about those healers who are diabetic themselves and need to eat regularly for health reasons? If healing is about energy, then why does what's happening in the body of the healer matter anyway? Surely it doesn't? What eventually offered me a dose of reality in this scenario was a friend who jokingly said to me, "I'm sure Jesus wouldn't have said to the leper, 'I'm sorry, I can't heal you right now, I've just had my lunch,' would he?"

She was absolutely right, but it illustrates how naïve and trusting I was in my teacher at that time. I remember feeling discouraged and disappointed for quite a while, partly because in one respect, I was always encouraged by her to explore and investigate my own relationship to the Spirit World, to ask questions and to evaluate the answers; but if those answers didn't match her understanding, then I was wrong. This inconsistency made me doubt her knowledge and skills, but thankfully I was inspired to eventually be my own authority, but not until I'd chosen to listen to my own instincts, trust the Spirit World, and educate myself about the subject separately and then finally to leave the healing group.

These tales, along with many other stories that students are taught, have no basis of truth, and only serve to create fear, disharmony and limitations within their minds. This fear and conflict, in turn, will limit their awareness because it places the student into their own mind rather than into their awareness, something we'll explore more in the next chapter.

The link between us and the Spirit World is a delicate one, and there are many influences that will affect how strong our connection is and what we can experience through it. When we begin our development, there is already uncertainty, lack of confidence and doubt. We hyper-examine everything; we hold on to what we receive, often trying to understand it before we even speak it; and very often we're only using a small part of the awareness we have available to us. Everything we experience as students needs to be encouraged to develop more fully.

What I've recognised over twenty-five years as a medium is that, like the bud of the flower, when the inner and outer conditions are right, the flower opens and grows into what it's destined to become. If we provide time, opportunity and openness, then we set the foundations for the Spirit World to blend with us and start to build the framework of our relationship together. Once these things are in place and in harmony with each other, we can truly allow our unique expression of mediumship to unfold.

Over the next few chapters, we'll look in detail at each element of the inner and outer conditions, which are supportive of not only the development of your mediumship, but also the practice of good-quality evidential mediumship and how important it is also to take care of your spiritual self whilst doing so. Some of the chapters will contain techniques or practices you can employ to enhance particular aspects of your spiritual work, and some will be reflective in nature.

The inner conditions of mediumship are really about what's going on within us; they are internal aspects of ourselves that we have a degree of control and influence over, and they directly impact our awareness. Through education, experience and committed practise working with these elements, we will experience a beneficial effect, not only in the accuracy of the evidence we receive but also in building confidence in ourselves and learning to trust the route our spiritual work takes. They are the keys to elevating your mediumship.

> Inner conditions – MIND, POWER, CONNECTION, BREATHING.

The outer conditions of mediumship are about the external aspects of your experience of mediumship. These elements are the aspects to be mindful of whilst working, as they directly support the inner conditions. These conditions are specifically techniques and practices you can employ to expand your awareness of the Spirit World, further enhance the inner conditions and also support you in your spiritual growth.

> Outer conditions – PEOPLE, ENVIRONMENT, LANGUAGE, EXPRESSION.

I believe it was Gordon Higginson who stated that 'your mediumship will be a reflection of you', and it's with that in mind that we will take a look at the first of the inner elements that will affect your mediumship the most: the mind.

INNER
CONDITIONS

CHAPTER 10

MIND

One of the most neglected areas of mediumship development is personal development, i.e. an examination of the self. We spend time and effort looking to the Spirit World to give to us but spend very little time looking at what we're offering to them. Mediumship is an emotional experience, filtered by the mind of medium; that is to say, what we hold within us will influence, affect and be reflected in our mediumship. In fact, what manifests in our communication with the Spirit World is either a reflection of them or a reflection of us.

In the earlier chapter on experiential mediumship, we looked at how some of these experiences and qualities can be incredibly helpful to the Spirit World, yet it is also important to understand that some aspects of ourselves can be detrimental to the Spirit World and the communications, and detract from the medium we wish to be.

Ideally, the medium moves into and is held by the power, and as the medium is so held, their conscious mind alters from being fully present, engaged and aware of their physical senses, to being an observer of the information coming from the Spirit communicator. As the communicators move into the presence of the medium, evidence is 'transmitted' through the auric (energy) field of the medium into their awareness. The conscious mind of the medium 'watches' this but doesn't interfere with it; they let it pass through and don't consciously think about it or analyse it. Whilst the medium's conscious mind moves out slightly, the subconscious and unconscious parts of the mind are closer to the surface. Because the conscious mind is not fully engaged and the subconscious mind is the most dominant during Spirit communication, this is often why mediums don't always remember what they have said to their recipients, unless they remind us afterwards.

We're usually very aware of what we're thinking in any given moment, but we're not always aware of the information that's held within our subconscious and unconscious mind. Ordinarily the content within these parts of the mind is hidden from our full awareness and usually comes up only when there is some sort of 'trigger'. These are the parts of the mind where the potential to sabotage the process of mediumship occurs, because of the 'filters' we hold within us. These filters can easily affect everything that takes place within the communication, from the types of evidence the medium is open to, even to the types of communicators they attract from the Spirit World. These 'filters' can also influence their ability to receive and communicate with the Spirit World at all.

The Oxford English Dictionary's definition of the word 'filter' states, "Process or assess (items) in order to reject those that are unwanted." This processing or assessing of information takes place in all aspects of the mind of the medium to some degree, but mostly operates in the background, often without them being aware of it. Some of the things we filter are very obvious, conscious and we're aware of them, and sometimes they're hidden and are buried away in our unconscious; they are rooted in difficult experiences or painful emotions. The filters we take into our psychic and mediumistic connections include:

1. Unresolved issues of the medium.
2. Prejudices of the medium (racism, homophobia, etc.).
3. The medium's beliefs/perceptions of the Spirit World and the process of mediumship.
4. The 'I'm not good enough' stuff.

UNRESOLVED ISSUES OF THE MEDIUM

We all have unresolved issues; we know them, but we may be reluctant to look at them. These are the experiences that make us have various physical reactions, such as increased heart rate or anxiety in the pit of the stomach when we think about them. It could be the pain of losing someone; the memory of being hurt; the guilt, anger and shame we sometimes feel about ourselves as a result of those things.

We often work really hard to defend ourselves from the pain of those experiences so that we don't feel them again; we avoid talking about the experience, and we deny and avoid feeling any associated emotions so that we can feel free and safe. We distract ourselves, we pretend we're OK, we do affirmations, engage in behaviours that we believe will move us further away from the upsetting experiences. Sometimes this is a conscious choice, but mostly it isn't – certainly regarding childhood traumas and experiences, the painful experiences are pushed into the unconscious mind, never to see the light of day again, so we don't always remember the details and can therefore live beyond the 'wound'.

When we move into our mediumship, we enter into a slightly more vulnerable state because our subconscious and unconscious experiences are closer to the surface and are therefore more likely to be re-experienced than at any other time. If some of your experiences are similar to an aspect of evidence that the Spirit communicator wishes to bring, the protectiveness of the conscious mind will filter it out so it doesn't disable the medium and put them into a crisis as they relive and re-experience their own stuff.

For example, if your dad had died of a heart attack and you didn't get to say goodbye, that pain is still alive within you, and if you haven't worked through the grief, it could compromise your mediumship. Your mind needs to 'protect' you, so it may mean that in your mediumship you block from the Spirit World all dads, everyone who's died from a heart attack or those who didn't get to say goodbye, because for you to experience those things again in your mediumship would bring up your past pain, and as a result, this could severely compromise your mediumship and put you into crisis.

PREJUDICES OF THE MEDIUM

All of us like to think that we are spiritually minded, loving, and accepting of everyone and everything without prejudice, but the truth is we all hold some form of prejudice or stereotyping. Common forms of prejudice are:

- Racism.
- Sexism.
- Ageism.
- Religious prejudice.
- Xenophobia.

Stereotyping of people, ideas, and objects is actually a very normal way in which we categorise the world so that we can navigate through it simply and easily. It is how we find our friends and avoid our perceived enemies. Prejudices are usually borne out of stereotypical experiences, usually our own, but they are sometimes handed down to us from our parents or society, and they can be positive or negative. Regardless of how they manifest, the root of prejudice comes from the concept of being separate from a person's idea of what is 'normal.'

Obviously, we are all unique – difference can't be avoided. Certainly, as a medium, our job is to deliver information that demonstrates the uniqueness and individuality of those loved ones who have passed away. However, if, as a medium, you hold a prejudice against a particular section of society, demographic, culture or ethnicity, this could result in you unconsciously blocking out anyone in your mediumship who carries the things you're prejudiced about. If you have issues with gay people on this side of life, then it's very likely you wouldn't experience a communicator who was gay when living.

MEDIUMS' BELIEFS AND PERCEPTIONS OF THE SPIRIT WORLD AND THE PROCESS OF MEDIUMSHIP

What do you believe about the Spirit World? Where is it? Who gets in and who doesn't? How do people communicate? Do you go to your first or second husband or wife when you die? These are just a few of the questions which we should ask ourselves and the Spirit World as we unfold our awareness. The wonderful thing about our mediumship reflecting us is that our awareness will also conform to the beliefs we hold about it. I remember watching a medium demonstrate at my local church, and she began the demonstration by saying, "If you died in a normal way, with cancer, a heart attack or a stroke, you go to the Spirit World no problem. If you died in any other way and died before your time, you go to a waiting room in the Spirit World until what would have been the time you should have passed over."

How does it feel to read that? Can you imagine how that sounded to the audience member whose son had committed suicide, or whose daughter had been murdered? Or to the parents who'd never been before and were hoping to hear from their twin sons who'd been killed in an accident? I can't even imagine the horror and distress this would have caused them. What was interesting about the subsequent demonstration was that the only people who'd communicated through the medium that night were little old ladies who'd died in their beds at a ripe old age, and men who 'lived well' and died naturally.

Whether it's about the Spirit World, the process of communication, how it works and why it doesn't, or about bigger beliefs such as God, religion, love, what's normal and what isn't, our awareness and sensitivity will be affected by those beliefs. We must periodically examine what we think, what we feel and what we know, and be open to learning from our experiences and inviting in new ones. I always say that everything I've ever needed to know about life and myself has been brought to me through a person or an experience. By being open to listening, by being willing to be challenged, we evolve and as we evolve as a person, so does the phenomena of our mediumship and how it's expressed.

'NOT GOOD ENOUGH' STUFF.

As an eighteen-year-old medium, I fought so hard to be 'right'. It was so important to me that everyone I spoke with believed my truth about the Spirit World being real. Because of this, when I was faced with someone who didn't, I would be offended or upset with them. How could they NOT believe me? Being humble wasn't easy in the early days; my mediumship was always the biggest thing in my world and I needed to show it to everyone. When I'd initially begun to take demonstrations, I was simply very grateful to be invited to demonstrate and was only too willing to go; I loved to serve the Spirit World. My ego also enjoyed my working for Spirit too, as it believed what everyone said to it about how great a medium Darren was, how amazing the evidence was and how Darren as a person must be so special to have so much ability at such a young age. It needed and wanted to believe the praise because it had never been so affirmed in all its life. The truth is that the foundation of my mediumship was built on the need it fulfilled within me. It was one of the very few times in my young life that I felt good, right, needed and valued. I identified with the belief that I was somehow better because of the mediumship; I felt inadequate and that made me egotistical.

The ego is the part of you that thinks 'IT' is something of value separate from everyone and everything else. It also means that you might:

- Get easily offended.
- Need to be right.
- Need to win or be the best.
- Need to feel superior.
- Need to have more or be more.
- Define yourself because of your achievements.
- Define yourself on the basis of your reputation.
- Define yourself by your associations with other people.

When in the grip of an 'ego trip', you are fully identifying with your self and are therefore likely to display all or some of the above behaviours, and hold certain beliefs and use particular language.

The belief in inadequacy isn't just about how we see ourselves based on our earlier experiences. If we identify with a thought or belief that as a developing medium we can't do it, we're not good enough, right enough, spiritual enough, clever enough or any other kind of 'enough', then we manifest the experience. Howard Falco, in his book *I Am*, states that, "The ego's desire is to turn the beliefs about itself into the experience of itself."

None of the filters I've mentioned are immoveable blocks. They are not fixed; they move, they disappear, they show up sometimes and not at others, but by the very nature of them they act as a 'saboteur' of information in the mediumistic state. Undertaking personal development and self-awareness classes, or counselling or psychotherapy, actually helps to reduce the impact of our filters because, by bringing the unconscious experiences into our conscious awareness, we can become free of their influence. When we don't resist, deny or avoid looking at those parts of us, not only do we get the benefit of psychological and emotional healing, we also 'unlock' the filter and thereby open ourselves up to more of the Spirit World. Regardless of which practice of self-awareness you engage in, the ONLY antidote to moving out of our ego, inadequacy, and the associated emotions and behaviours is to develop and cultivate empathy, for ourselves and everyone else.

CHAPTER 11

POWER

"The more you lose yourself in something bigger than yourself, the more energy you will have."

Norman Vincent Peale (Clergyman) 1893–1993

In the early years of my development, not once did I ever hear anyone talk about 'the power' in relation to mediumship. I was never told to sit in it, tap in to it, build it, speak with it or stand in it, and if anyone had mentioned 'the power', I wouldn't have even known where to find it anyway! Even now, when you ask a medium, "What is the power?", you'll get differing answers about what it is, what it does and where it is. What I knew back then, without knowing its name, was that in my connections to the Spirit World there was always some kind of force that was sustaining me as I worked. I could feel an expansion, a growing sense of being 'held', and there was a faint but distinct experience of being 'more' in their presence. I noticed that I would feel greater compassion, more loved and that it came from *within* me – it wasn't external.

Even when I wasn't demonstrating active mediumship, but just sitting within an open circle or at home with myself, I could feel this presence. I would sit quietly and yet I'd become aware that there was a kind of noise – not a physical or external sound, but an inner resonance which, when I focussed on it, became all I would notice. The more I observed it, the closer I got to it, until eventually there was no separation between me and it; then came a feeling of oneness. The closest I can come to explaining it in earthly terms is that it felt like being in a sea of love where I could feel its movement, see its flow, know its thoughts and yet felt safe in it because I knew that it loved me. The more I held awareness of this, over time it became more evident to me that I was more than just Darren. Darren is my identity, but it wasn't and isn't who I am at my core.

The concept that there is a power relating to mediumship initially came from the Spirit World through a trance communication in the presence of the wonderful medium Glyn Edwards. The communicator stated that 'sitting in the power' was the way to build our awareness of them and that this power, put very simply, is love. I've heard many definitions of the power over the years and many stories about how best to tap in to it. The Spirit World's definition of it being love is, without question, the only one which resonates with me. Love IS the power of the soul. Within that power is held the potential from which *all* things manifest. It's the same potential that presents to anyone who is inspired (or rather, compelled!) to follow their passion, whether it be music, medicine, art, engineering or any other such love. As I've discussed earlier in this book, mediumship is also a potential that is held within the soul. It cannot be learned, it must be revealed, and as it does so its desire is to heal and to elevate the consciousness of others. The experience of mediumship has a therapeutic benefit and can help to heal dis-ease in people, especially those who are grieving the loss of love they perceive through death. Mediumship is a reminder to the observer that there is no death, love can't die, and when we know a reunion with our loved one is inevitable, we can continue living with and eventually beyond the wound that grief creates within us.

Hopefully, armed with this new-found knowledge, a recipient of evidential mediumship would then go on to explore their own spirituality by sitting to identify themselves as Spirit, and maybe eventually to reach out to the Spirit World themselves too. It's not uncommon for people who have received clear evidence from their loved ones to want to explore their own awareness, often in the hope that they can experience their own loved one's presence directly. Our awareness of our being, and there being something 'more', is often preceded by some form of suffering or loss, and one of my favourite quotes regarding this is from Rumi, a Persian poet and Sufi: "The wound is the place where the light enters you."

Firstly, I need to make it clear that 'sitting in the power' and 'building the power' are two very different disciplines. When we sit in the power we are sitting in full, conscious awareness that we ARE love, that we ARE Spirit and soul combined, and that we ARE God (not the religious version of God!). For some, this is a huge concept for the mind to grasp without feeling in some way blasphemous or egotistical, but this revelation is not of the mind; it's soul-inspired, and there's no need to fear it. When we sit with this knowing, it makes ALL this available to us, including those in the Spirit World. The act of sitting in the power actually 'spiritualises' us, meaning it reminds us of our true selves, and the more we identify as this, the more we become a demonstration of all that love is. Not only does this help to improve the consciousness and awareness of those around us, but it also does so on a greater scale, to humanity at large. I can always tell those mediums who sit in the power regularly because they exude love; I would also say they 'practise what they preach', but then these people also have no need to preach either – they are just a walking demonstration of love.

As you will probably realise by now, 'building the power' is impossible, as this power is already immeasurable and infinite. We cannot 'build' anything that is already full; it would therefore be more accurate to say that we're building our *experience* of the power. It's also true to say that we can never *lose* the power either. Often, when mediums are coming to the end of their demonstrations, they will say, "The power has dropped," which suggests there's only a limited amount and it can 'run out'. Again, we *can* lose awareness of it, or our connection to it as our mind interferes, or our physical body demands our attention, but the power itself doesn't ever diminish. In the practice of mediumship, the power not only fuels the connection, but it also sustains the medium, supports the communicator and upholds the process of communication. I've heard teachers say that you have to stand still when demonstrating, otherwise you'll move out of the power. Let me be clear: there can be no separation between you and it because you ARE the power. Where you move, it moves; where you stand, it stands. It does not occupy a separate physical space to you; there is no portal, or 'hotspot', to the power that is outside of you.

So, can we work with our mediumship without sitting in the power as a regular practice? I would have to say yes, but I would also advise against it. The process of regularly sitting gives us the experience of surrendering to the power, therefore helping our conscious mind and ego to move out of our immediate awareness, which is vital when we come to working with our mediumship. Once we identify with ourselves as a spiritual being, and allow the power of mediumship to be present, then our awareness of and sensitivity to the Spirit World is enhanced. In doing so, then the communications are not only filled with evidence and love, but the medium's energy levels, awareness and focus are also maintained. Sitting regularly also benefits those in the Spirit World, as it gives them the opportunity to blend with us, to learn the communication process, as well as offering us their love and inspiration as we sit; this in, and of, itself is incredibly restorative.

SITTING IN THE POWER EXERCISE

With any form of meditative practice, especially with sitting in the power, ensure there are no distractions for at least twenty minutes, turn off phones and find a quiet place. Bodily comfort should be made a priority, as any form of discomfort within the body will make demands on your attention. This involves the mind, which may disconnect you from your awareness. Also, sit upright rather than lying down, as the association with lying down and sleep may be too much for your body to resist! Once an upright sitting position is held, it's important initially to keep the mind tethered and held in a certain 'place'. If not, it's like an excitable puppy – easily distracted and likely to cause chaos! A really good way to do this is to physically stare at an object; this object must not have any associations with it that could stimulate your memories, nor should it be anything you could attach meaning to. For this reason, avoid looking at photographs, religious icons, crystals or any such thing; ideal things are light switches, marks on the wall, etc. Then stare, and keep staring; the mind will want to look away to find a distraction, but resist and keep staring. Keep staring until you feel an inner point when you feel it's 'time' to close your eyes, and when you feel it's right to do so, gently close your eyes. At this point, the conscious mind is surrendering the need to be in control. Then focus on your breathing; just notice the natural rhythm and flow of each breath without trying to change it. Observe the way the breath flows in, and out of your body with only a pause between each breath. Count each element; breathe in, pause, breathe out, pause. If you find yourself getting distracted, focus again on your breath and become the observer of it.

Where do the pauses, the space between each breath, live in your body? Where do you feel they are? Look for the pauses, notice them and notice also that in the pause, the body is still, almost at rest. Focus more on the pauses and look for the stillness in them; it's in this stillness that your awareness lives – this is the way to the soul. Keep focussed on the feeling of stillness and know that the more attention you give it, the more aware of it you'll become. Sit in this space, noticing the pause and the stillness contained within it.

Your mind may wish to make this space tangible to you by attaching an image to this feeling; it could be the image of the sun or moon, the flame of a candle, or even a light bulb. If it does, allow your breath to influence the light; every breath in, strengthens and makes the light brighter, and every breath out, like blowing up a balloon, makes it bigger. Let the out breath push out the light each time, feeling the sense of stillness increase as you do so; watch it increase under the influence of your breath until the room is filled with this light. Notice as it grows, your awareness of it grows too, and in doing so, you may start to experience seeing or feeling colours. Watch the colours and be curious about how they might feel, continue to observe them with curiosity. Allow the presence and awareness of this energy to captivate you, and move with it as it moves, and observe as it fills the space around you. Look for the feeling in its presence and be curious about that. The more you identify with this light, the more aware and attuned to it you'll become. Do you have a sense of how this energy moves; does it have a flow or a pattern to it? Does it have a sound to it? Be curious about it and be open to its reality. Notice how it moves, how it looks, how it sounds and how it feels. After a period of time, the sitting will generally come to its natural conclusion. Initially the mind finds it difficult to keep out of the experience and will often try to distract or sabotage you. However, with consistent practise, the mind learns to stay put and eventually becomes the observer of the experience.

The experience of sitting in the power will deepen, as will the recognition that the power is not separate from you. Most likely, there will be subtle differences each time you sit and there will also be a temptation for your mind to attach meaning to any images or sensations that you experience. As much as possible, focus on the feeling aspect of your awareness, and if distracted, always go back to the breath to 'stabilise' your awareness and reconnect you to the stillness. Once you're able to fully identify with this power, combined with a clear intent, it's then possible to move into the experience of connecting to those in the Spirit World.

To get the full benefit of sitting in the power, consistency really is important. The mind will always try to rationalise any experience that involves us via our psychic awareness or spiritual senses, and so it needs to learn to become less involved. If you're able to devote thirty minutes every day to this practice, it will soon start to become more familiar. Once it becomes familiar, the mind will be less involved in trying to sabotage the experience. It's very common for students to feel like they're getting nowhere initially, and the discipline of sitting is really helpful to enable students to monitor their progress. If at first you don't succeed...

This is a written form of the exercise I deliver on my CD *The Light Within*.

CHAPTER 12

CONNECTION

How do we define 'connection' in terms of mediumship and psychic work, and how can we validate it when it's occurred? When using mediumship and the intuitive arts, especially when demonstrating in a public arena, the importance of communicating information which can be validated is huge. Mediums and psychics rise and fall due to the quality and clarity of the evidence they deliver, and unless we receive responses from the recipient, there is no other objective way to assess the connection. The chair people at our mediumship demonstrations often say we need validation and confirmation from our recipients for us to work well. We seem to rely on the recipients' responses to know how well we're doing. As mediums, we look to validate our experience of mediumship in a very external way. We ask the recipients to reply with 'yes' or 'no' to the statements we offer. But is it really necessary? When we look to validate our *internal* experience from an *external* perspective, we're always going to be at the mercy of others. When we also *demand* that recipients validate our evidence, then in essence we're not fully trusting our own connection.

A connection can be defined as the linking of at least two people or things. In working both as a psychic and as a medium, there is a point A and a point B. As a medium, your point of connection is between you and the Spirit World. As a psychic, it's with another person, place or thing. The intent with both mediumship and psychic connections is that you have access through your sensitivity to the experience of something or someone separate to you. As always, it is the *intent* that moves us to experience the *content*, and whatever you focus your attention on, your awareness will move towards.

PSYCHIC CONNECTION

There are two types of psychic connection; both depend upon there being a particular 'object' to read. The first type I call a *subjective* connection, meaning that the person or thing you're reading is sharing the same space that you are in, i.e. the client is with you or you're psychically holding an object, etc. The second method is an *objective* connection, which is where the person, object or place you're reading isn't in the same physical space as you, i.e. they're in another country and so on.

With a *subjective* connection, the psychic focusses their intent on the person or object, moves into their sensitivity and states their intent to understand the experiences of the person the connection relates to. When using my psychic faculty, I state my intent, focus on the recipient and then I experience a form of expansion where my sensitivity almost reaches out towards the person. Once focussed, I then have access to the recipient's experiences, and as my conscious, logical mind moves out, I'm left feeling their experiences as if they were my own.

Alternatively, with an *objective* connection, there is also a focus, a point of connection that takes place away from the physical presence of the psychic. Whilst it is our intent that defines the outcome of the reading, when giving an objective reading, often psychics will ask for a name or date of birth to act as a focal point for their awareness. When I've given psychic readings at distance, I hold the name, date of birth or another focal point within my mind and I 'feel' it. I hold it close to me and I adopt a curiosity about the person, place or thing.

Again, once my sensitivity increases and my conscious, logical mind moves out, then I start to experience images, feelings, sounds and impressions related to the target or focus. With both methods of connecting, you're reading the energy or auric field surrounding the person, place or thing.

Everything we have ever experienced in our lives, including all our thoughts and feelings, stay within our energy field forever. Every loss, every joy and every hurt sit there, and regardless of whether it's been healed or not, the memory of it remains and can be read by a psychic. That isn't to say that we are walking around as an open book for any medium or psychic to access.

If, for example, there are experiences in our lives we don't want to reveal, then the auric field will also reflect that in how it behaves. It will not reveal what the mind doesn't want to release, and this is especially true when there are experiences regarding shame or guilt. Using the example of someone who has been abused, a psychic may well get a sense of a trauma at a certain point in their life, and peripheral feelings of the experience, but because the client is still experiencing shame, guilt or denial about that experience, the aura may 'shield' the psychic from knowing the details of what they went through. That shielding doesn't occur when reading an object or a place, because unlike people, objects cannot create defence mechanisms which operate in the same way that people can. In fact, when reading for people who seemed to be defensive, fearful or guarded, I would often ask to hold an object of theirs, as this bypassed some parts of their shielding process. As a side note, when doing psychometry, where we're able to read the memory of the object's life and its wearer, those objects such as watches or chains that have been worn over a pulse often gave greater impressions. I think it's partly due to the fact that everything we go through in life impacts the circulatory system, and our pulse rate changes according to every emotion and state of consciousness. It would, therefore, make sense that when an object has been worn over these areas, there is a greater 'charge' of energy and, therefore, information transferred onto it.

MEDIUMSHIP CONNECTION

A person who demonstrates an evidential connection to the Spirit World is called a medium. The keyword here is *evidential*, meaning there has to be a component where the reality of the individual who has passed over is demonstrated through the accuracy of information the medium gives.

That is to say, you cannot claim to be a medium and then give nothing evidential. Over many years I have witnessed all manner of things passed off as evidence of the Spirit World, which at best was whimsical and at worst was utter nonsense. Unicorns, archangels, aliens, and all manner of other mythological beasts and beings have been given from mediums under the guise of mediumship, and yet none of these things can be proven.

Likewise, statements such as, "She loves you," "She's proud of you," or "She says you're kind," are all very nice to hear, but as we've already said, they don't constitute evidence of life after death. We have a responsibility to the Spirit World, and to the legacy of those wonderful evidential mediums who've gone before us, to demonstrate the reality of the Spirit World through the strength and authenticity of our connection to it.

In order to make a connection, we need a point A and a point B, and if we're point A, we need to know how to access point B, and to do that we need to know where to focus our attention in order to begin. A common question I hear is, "Where is the Spirit World?" Let's make a very earthy comparison to illustrate the point. The room you're now sitting in is filled with communication. Look around. It's filled with TV signals, radio waves, mobile phone signals; there are text messages buzzing around, waiting to be delivered. There is information whizzing around you and yet you don't see it; you don't see it unless there's a receiver which is capable of connecting to the frequency of those unseen signals. Once we turn on the TV, answer the phone or switch on the radio, that 'world', which goes unseen without a receiver, starts to become tangible and real. A medium is also a receiver, but to the thoughts, feelings and communications from those who have passed away. So, when we can accept that, the answer to where the Spirit World is becomes very clear: it's right here, and our loved ones are ever-present, albeit on a different frequency and, for the most part, outside our awareness. When we make a connection or tune in through our sensitivity, whether it be consciously or otherwise, the reality of the Spirit World is apparent to us. This is also possible when giving a mediumship reading for someone at distance, over the internet, via email, by letter or any other 'medium'.

Students of mediumship often ask, "How do I know it's the Spirit World communicating?" and "How do I know I'm connected?"

Whenever we connect to the Spirit World, we shouldn't just rely on the evidence alone as an indicator of our connection. After all, our imagination can make up all sorts of wonderful stories that have nothing to do with the Spirit World! Regardless of the thoughts in our head, we must also be open to the *experience* and *feeling* of connection within us in the following ways:

Physical sensations –
temperature changes, sensations of pressure, feeling bigger or smaller, shivery feelings, palpitation-like sensation, tears.

Emotional changes –
feeling more loved or more loving. A welling up

of emotion from within, feelings of being held, supported and safe.

Psychological changes –
absence of thinking, no head chatter.

When we initially begin our mediumship unfoldment, any of the above sensations can present in a very tangible way and they're difficult to ignore. We often look for them and come to rely on them as indicators of connection, and then we worry when one day we don't have them! At the beginning of my mediumship I would know it was the Spirit World communicating because I would experience what felt like a second heartbeat in my abdomen. That was my 'sign' that I was connected, and it always preceded the evidence from a communicator. After a period of time, and when I'd learned to recognise the presence of a communicator and to connect intuitively without the thump of the heartbeat, the signs of connection appeared to be less tangible. I think as trust started to build in my awareness and my connection, I didn't need those 'big' physical signs so much, but even now, my amplified emotional state and also how my mind behaves when I'm connected remain the same.

So, as you can see, the only difference in psychic connections compared to mediumship connections is the origin of the information; how we experience them is the same. In both faculties, we can see, hear, feel, smell, taste and know information, but the feeling is definitely different; one is concerned with and is from a Spirit communicator, and the other isn't. It's also important to understand that if we accept that all information is held within the energy field of our recipients, then it's also important to accept that it's very possible to read the memory of someone's death through the recipient's energy field too and *not* get that information from the actual Spirit Communicator. The only way we can be sure of the origin as mediums is to reach out to feel the living presence of that loved one in our connection to them.

When reading the memory of the experience through the aura, we can still give highly specific information, but their presence won't be felt by the medium, and nor will it be felt by the recipient or audience either. When working as a medium, it's important to recognise that everything you experience, including how you behave, contains an evidential quality to it. How you stand, how you move, the flick of your hair, even the way you speak may be aspects of the communicator; it's therefore important that our mind maintains an 'observer' role so that this can be identified when it happens.

Why is it so important to know the difference, and how can we ensure both dynamics are clearly defined? Firstly, it's about honesty and authenticity. If we are advertised as an evidential medium, then that is what we should offer. If it's an evening of psychic readings, then that's what we do. Regardless of whether the audience know the difference or not, WE should know. What that means for our awareness is that there is a clarity to it, it isn't scattered or unclear, it doesn't lack flow and, most importantly, it still retains its therapeutic potential and quality. By offering people a psychic reading under the guise of mediumship, you're potentially robbing the recipient (and the Spirit communicator!) of the opportunity to heal because the presence of their loved one isn't being communicated or even allowed through you. Conversely, if you're advertised as a psychic and someone comes along not expecting to hear from the 'dead', and you then launch into speaking about their departed great-aunt Marge, it could freak them out so much it sends them into the Spirit World to be with her!

The way that I operate with my awareness, especially when I'm demonstrating in public, is that I define the space between myself and the audience. I visualise an energetic 'wall' between us which affirms where my faculty as a medium ends and my faculty as a psychic begins. When I am in my mediumship, I'm very clear on feeling the presence of the communicator and also how the evidence presents. If, throughout the demonstration, there's an intuitive need for me to speak about the recipient's life, then my awareness gets gently moved into the energy of the recipient under the guidance and influence of the Spirit World, so I'm able to operate on that level. Affirming this space is a way that also insures I'm not likely to be influenced by the 'demand' of the audience. As I move into my sensitivity to the Spirit World, I'm also aware of the thoughts and feelings of the audience. An audience member demanding and wanting a communication could have the effect of pulling my awareness to them without the spirit people directing that communication. If my awareness is moved to the demanding audience member and into their aura, I always explain to them what's happening so that they are educated about the difference and also in the name of transparency. Just to make this clear, I'm defining the space of my *awareness*, and not defining the limit of the power of the Spirit within or around me. The power of love that comes through a medium in connection with the Spirit World fills the entire room; it knits and holds the audience in its embrace, ensuring the potential for them to feel the presence of the Spirit World, even if they don't receive a direct communication.

In relation to connection, I want to reiterate this point: it is that whatever we give our attention to, we move towards. In the search for a recipient's validation, and by constantly asking them to affirm the evidence, we sometimes focus a little too much on them and can inadvertently disconnect from the Spirit World. By doing so, we move into their space and then the connection moves into more of a psychic connection rather than a mediumistic one. People mistakenly think that a 'psychic message' is when the medium starts talking about earthly things such as, "You have a new washing machine," or, "You have a bad tooth," but in reality, how the dynamic is defined is not by the content held within it, but by the type of connection made in order to receive it.

CHAPTER 13

BREATHING

This might sound like an odd question, but have you noticed how you breathe lately? Have you observed how it changes according to what you're doing, how you're feeling and your state of mind? I feel sure you'll have noticed that it's different when you're meditating compared to when you're stressed at work or worried.

Sadly, stress is a natural part of modern life, and depending on the levels of stress we're experiencing, it can have hugely adverse effects on our physical and mental health. When we're experiencing a threat, or are feeling 'unsafe' in some way, our mind and body recognises it as stress. A little infrequent and irregular stress can be motivating and helpful – for example, for performance – but when it's over a long period or is intense, it can evolve into something far more damaging.

One of the ways we can navigate our way through stressful times is to use our breath consciously. Not only are there benefits to our health and well-being, but the quality of our breath and the pattern of it can also impact our awareness and sensitivity. To illustrate the point with reference to mediumship, it's important to look at our reactions when faced with any kind of stress.

Imagine you're about to stand in front of an audience of three hundred people, all of whom have paid £15 to attend, and you're the only medium on the bill. You're not feeling well to begin with – it's just some kind of cold or bug, nothing major, but you know it's taking your attention. Only three hours earlier, as you were ironing your shirt, you took a call from your mum to inform you that one of your family members had been murdered. Thirty minutes before your demonstration you arrive at the venue to a room full of people – some you know are probably already believers, some are sceptical and some of these might be very vocal. There is an air of expectation, almost of demand, in the air and you have no clue what you're going to say to anyone, or if you're even going to be able to receive any communication, because not only are you not feeling well, but you are also heartbroken. What if you stand up and you don't see, or hear, or feel a thing? How will you explain it? What if you do get information but no-one will accept it, or can accept it? The lights go down in the auditorium, you're introduced to the stage, the light goes up and on you walk...

Stress actually causes the body to tense up, and in so doing, we start to breathe a little more shallowly, and when this is sustained, the muscles around our chest begin to tighten. When we shallow breathe and breathe quickly through stress, we lower carbon dioxide levels, but oxygen levels in the blood become higher. The brain recognises this as more stress and we then start to feel fear – the process of feeling anxious has begun. As we become more fearful, we'll hold our breath in the belief that doing so will stop the emotions and sensations increasing – this actually traps the anxiety inside and further alters the blood chemistry. When we're in front of the public, we don't want them to see that we're struggling, so we pretend everything is OK. When this continues, we'll also begin to experience other symptoms and sensations: the physical sensations of suffocation, a rapid heartbeat, shortness of breath, dry mouth, shakiness, sweating and numb fingers. There are also psychological changes, such as confusion, a difficulty in thinking clearly, feeling detached and also changes in our perception of reality. Another thing that happens is that our physical senses become sharper because we're now in total fear of what is happening and what might happen, and we want to avoid the perceived threat (and the feelings), so we look for ways to 'escape' them.

Depending on how severely and how long this process lasts, it could eventually turn into a full-blown anxiety or panic attack. If at any point throughout this process we only breathed differently, our experience would change, our minds would calm, the physical sensations would subside and the anxiety or panic attack would gradually cease. Thankfully I had remembered this before I walked on stage that day.

What we know for certain about mediumship is that we move our awareness away from the physical world into the Spirit World. We hold it there to receive communication. To carry out this process efficiently, we need to give less attention to our thinking, to the information and to our physical senses. Our mind needs to be in a state of passivity rather than activity, and we also need to be free of emotional stress, especially anger or fear. By harnessing the power of our breath consciously, we can then move beyond the demands of the body, mind and emotions. If we can also accomplish this when we're actively using our awareness, then it will help us to stay connected.

In her autobiography *Adventures in the Supernormal: A Personal Memoir*, Irish medium Eileen Garrett explains how breath both controlled and influenced her awareness. She maintained that with different tempos of breathing, she experienced different phenomena in her mediumship, including clairaudience, clairvoyance, telepathy and precognition. Her experience also taught her that the acceleration of her breathing increased the power of these faculties.

This observation also mirrored my own experiences. Having undergone panic and anxiety attacks in my earlier years, I'm acutely aware that when my breathing pattern alters there is a corresponding change in my mind, my body and in my perception of reality. Thanks to cognitive behavioural therapy, I'm now able to employ techniques that prevent me getting to the point of a panic attack.

I've noticed that when I demonstrate mediumship publicly, my breathing pattern changes between each part of the service. It's slower during the prayer, deeper during the philosophy and faster during the mediumship demonstration. I've recognised that I can use and manipulate the breath when I need to deepen my awareness or to gain more clarity within the evidence.

For example, in the early years when I was given a piece of evidence from a communicator, I would attempt to make sense of it from my own logic or understanding. Invariably, my interpretation wasn't accurate, because I was too separate from it to truly understand and feel its significance. In an attempt to understand more, I needed to deepen my experience and awareness, and I learned that if I focussed on the image and used my breath to connect with it by 'breathing it closer', I would gain more clarity. I would use this technique when I wanted to find out more specific information such as names. It didn't always work, but it worked more often than not.

The use of our breath aids us in maintaining our awareness of the Spirit World and reaching for more specific information, whilst assisting in keeping our minds free of stress.

The more specific evidence we reach for in our awareness, the more likely we are to feel greater anxiety about the outcome. This reaching for more detail – whether it's names, addresses, how a person passed or other specifics – will cause us stress, because we know there's a greater 'risk' that we'll get the information wrong. It's at such times that using our breath consciously is our saviour.

I consciously use my breathing, specifically when a recipient says 'no' to any information that I deliver. There's no greater stress for a medium hearing a recipient say no, even more so when they say it more than three times in a row! We know we're going to hear it – mediums aren't infallible – but nos do have the potential to reduce us to a gibbering wreck.

When we're feeling mentally or physically stressed, we unconsciously hold our breath to suppress or avoid what we're feeling, and in so doing, we set off a whole chain reaction of events which causes us further stress; as a medium, stress is not your friend!

The antidote to the downward spiral that can come from hearing no are the following steps which you may find very helpful.

HANDLING NOS

- When you hear no, take a conscious breath.
- Acknowledge the no with a, "Thank you, let me help you understand."
- Using your breath, focus on and move closer to your Spirit communicator.
- Don't allow the recipient's no to move you away from what you 'know'.
- 'Follow' the evidence that evoked the no until you feel you can't get any more information.
- Ensure that you don't move into a 'need to be right' state; be honest if you're getting it wrong or feel that you're not with the right recipient.

Breathing consciously at these times will also keep the anxiety levels down within you so you don't become aroused. Arousal in this sense of the word means that you don't allow awareness of your own physiological and psychological state; if you do let yourselves get to this state, then it's often 'game over' for your non-physical awareness. When you use your breath to remain connected to your awareness, it also helps you to deepen your sensitivity. It's as easy as A, B, C:

Awareness = Breath + Connection

Once we become familiar with the situation we're in, we naturally start to feel less anxious and our breathing patterns will return to a healthier state. From this point, we don't need to 'consciously' breathe, other than when we wish to deepen our evidence or to manage the impact of no from a recipient.

Being a medium entails a huge amount of vulnerability, especially when we work in the public arena. It's perfectly normal to feel nervous, uncertain and sometimes overwhelmed.

The following exercise will help to calm the mind and still the body in preparation for your spiritual work:

1. Have your eyes open or closed throughout, whatever is most comfortable.
2. Take a long, slow breath in through your nose for a count of five.
3. Hold for a count of three.
4. Breathe out slowly, through the mouth, for a count of seven.
5. Do this for several minutes until you start to feel better.

OUTER
CONDITIONS

CHAPTER 14

PEOPLE

After what I felt had been a particularly evidential sitting, the recipient asked, "If my dad is *really* there, get him to tell you what I put on his grave..." My initial response was disappointment, then sadness. Even though his dad had worked SO hard to let his son know he was OK, it still wasn't enough for him. The reality is that when working with our mediumship, there is always an expectation. Granted, it isn't always voiced, but it's there, hidden beneath the sweet smile and the inevitable, "I'm really just open to whatever comes."

"Cauliflower," was the answer. His dad had never liked flowers and often said, "When I'm gone, the only flowers I want on my grave are cauliflowers." After hearing this, the sitter dissolved into tears and it was clear he then understood it was his dad communicating. I felt pleased, relieved and vindicated; however, just for a moment after his question it had put me into my head and into the belief I'd failed. Thankfully, I was able to maintain my connection to his dad, enabling me to receive the answer to his question, but it could have been a very different outcome.

I'm sure that recipients of our mediumship don't *mean* to be difficult or challenging, but the truth is that they can be, and I totally understand why. I can only imagine the desperation of a parent as they sit with a medium, wanting to know that their child has made it to the Spirit World and wanting reassurance that one day, they'll meet again. They *need* to be sure it's real, they want their pain to ease, and in their desperation they're not willing to let their guards down easily and risk any more suffering.

By offering our mediumistic communications, we are presenting to our sitter an opportunity to heal some part of their grief, and in doing so, it often means they are required to look their pain squarely in the face. This is challenging and daunting enough to do in private, but inviting people do this in a very public area is much more difficult.

Defensiveness and resistance are therefore things we must accept we're going to be faced with in mediumship, and whilst it may not always be demonstrated as overtly as the 'cauliflower' sitter, it's almost certainly likely to present.

The impact of this on the 'sensitive' can be huge. As we sit in front of our clients and recipients using our sensitivity to feel the Spirit World, we are also likely to be sensitive to the energies being focussed on us from this side of life too. The smiling sceptic, the grieving parent, the curious but scared teenager, the man who sits with his arms crossed, the woman who refuses to make eye contact, the people who refuse to speak and those who book a sitting using a name other than their own; all of these have the potential to negatively influence us.

As mediums, we have a foot in both worlds and as such are fully aware of the influences from both sides of life. Of course, we need to engage with our recipients, but we must also be mindful that we never lose our awareness of those communicating from the Other World. This isn't an easy practice to adhere to, especially when we're being faced with some form of expectation or demand.

In fact, whenever I ask a student why they want to be a medium, invariably they say, "Because I want to help people." The problem with this statement is that the potential medium is already making the process *and* the effect of their mediumship about meeting their own need. As the medium, of course you will *want* to please the client, to make them happy and to meet their need. You may also want to ensure they recommend you to their friends, give you a good review and share their positive experience on social media.

Generally speaking, when our motivation to practice mediumship is the fulfilling of a need within us, we'll place too much of our awareness on the sitter because we require their validation. We look for signs that we are getting it right and we notice our sitter's every movement, attempting to interpret it as we desperately search for validation. This will have a detrimental impact on our mediumship as we move our awareness away from the needs of the Spirit World and project them onto the sitter or even onto ourselves.

We must never lose awareness of the Spirit World; without their involvement we fail to be the medium. Regardless of what's going on in the heart, mind and energy of the recipient, the *only* way we can be influenced by them in our work is if we give them too much attention and awareness. I think a healthier motivation for doing this work is the need to blend with the Spirit World, for its own sake and without an agenda. Being free from any attachment to an outcome, a healing and even a benefit for anyone, enables us to stay in our connection with Spirit.

There is something remarkable that happens to people once the reality of the Spirit World has been demonstrated. In 2019 I had been asked to teach at a seminar for the International Spiritualist Federation in East Anglia, and as part of the seminar, I was to take a demonstration. The day arrived and I was anxious before I took the platform, but that wasn't particularly unusual – nerves are pretty normal under those circumstances. As the demonstration began, I was incredibly aware of the Spirit World; the communicators were very clear to me and the evidence appeared to be getting clearer and clearer as the demonstration progressed. The evidence included full names of communicators, addresses given in other languages and personal information far beyond anything I'd ever experienced before. The evidence was unusual, precise and undisputable. I was aware that my consciousness was expanding, a sensation that wasn't unusual to me when I demonstrated, and I'd learned by now to just go with this feeling and allow myself to be 'held' by them; the flow of accurate evidence continued. There came a point when the only reality I had was of those in the Spirit World. Of course, I was aware that I was on the platform in front of one hundred people, but all I could see, feel and hear was the Spirit World. The audience's reactions were profound and immediate; there were tears from recipients, shouts of joy and I could feel the audience was enjoying the demonstration. Around an hour into the ninety-minute demonstration, something changed; I could sense a difference in the audience. I was still very much held by the Other World and the evidence continued, and yet I felt the audience had withdrawn from the process; it felt like the energy of the room had suddenly depleted. My awareness of this caused my mind to become more present as I started to question what was happening. I questioned whether, in this state of not being fully present, I said something inappropriate and had annoyed the audience? I started searching the audience for signs of what was wrong. I even turned to the chairperson to check his reactions; he was no different, so clearly I hadn't done or said anything I shouldn't have – that was a relief, at least!

The demonstration came to an end and I felt troubled as I didn't know what on earth had happened. I asked several people afterwards and they said there *was* a difference in the atmosphere, although they reassured me I hadn't done anything wrong. But something *had* happened, and whatever it was, I'd allowed it to take me from one state of mediumship into another, and the change in atmosphere had enough power to pull my mind back into the experience. Whenever something happens like this, it's important for me to sit with the Spirit World to learn from them about what happened. As I got back to my room, I sat to ask those whom I work with and was blown away by their response.

When a medium demonstrates mediumship publicly, the audience's focus is on the medium and they experience the Spirit World as something separate to them. They're engaged with the medium and give their attention to the process but continue to be separate to it, unless or until the medium addresses them directly. At this point they're possibly open to the reality of the Spirit World, and if the evidence from their loves ones is strong and clear enough, they will fully engage in the process and gain benefit from it.

Once they've received proof, they will then move into a place of introspection and internal focus as they remember and relive their experience of their loved ones. It was explained to me that once the reality of the Spirit World is demonstrated to an audience who are all captivated by the evidence and the presence of the Spirit World, then the audience as a whole also moves into this same introspective place because '...if their loved ones have survived death, then so must mine'. This mass inner contemplation affected the atmosphere as they became focussed internally and less focussed on the outside experience being demonstrated. This made complete sense to me, but I'd never experienced it to this degree before. What *was* interesting is that I had defaulted to the belief it was my fault, that in some way I'd done a bad thing – clearly this was something I would need to look at. It was the story I'd told myself about this experience that altered my experience of the Spirit World that night.

That's the only reason people can affect us as mediums, because of the story we tell ourselves about them. They can't 'block' us unless we believe they can; they can't disconnect us from the Spirit World unless we inadvertently buy into that belief. By all means notice changes, in you and in the recipients, certainly observe how the audience respond, but that's all – just observe it and don't go telling yourself a negative story, or your mediumship will suffer because of it.

CHAPTER 15

ENVIRONMENT

Regardless of what our job entails, our workspace has the power to influence us, either positively or in negative ways. I think most of us have experienced sensing a 'vibe' upon entering a room and we use expressions such as 'you could have cut the atmosphere with a knife' to describe how it feels in a space where there has been an argument or tension. Atmosphere is tangible, and whether you regard yourself as psychic or not, it's noticeable. Have you ever observed that when you walk into a church, there is a definite urge to speak softly and quietly? It's almost as if there is a presence in the space inspiring your behaviour; that is what atmosphere does – it inspires thinking, feeling and behaviour. What atmosphere can also do is inspire us to imagine how we might feel if we are exposed to it.

Crumlin Road Gaol in Belfast is a former jail, which held prisoners for 150 years, in which seventeen executions were carried out; the last execution took place in 1961. The prison housed inmates from many areas of society, including some members of the IRA. After closing its doors in 1996, it stood empty for many years until, after its restoration in 2012, it was re-opened as a tourist attraction and conference centre. Although it had been converted, huge portions of the prison were kept intact, including the execution chamber and the cells. The atmosphere inside reflected its history. Walking through the corridors, you couldn't help but imagine the despair and the pain that its inmates would have felt. There was a feeling of hopelessness, even madness. As we entered the execution chamber, there was still a palpable feeling of fear in the air. I shuddered at the pain inflicted within those walls. Later that evening, myself and two other mediums would demonstrate in the former canteen.

I believed that the energy in any room contains the potential to influence my awareness and because I knew this, I felt nervous. Would it actually be possible to bring messages of hope to anyone in an environment where the atmosphere was steeped in such misery? Walking into that room, I couldn't avoid my mind dwelling on the people who'd been executed, and thinking about those who'd been denied joy, could never find peace, those who held on to their anger and those who had a desire to hurt others. The room contained a capacity audience waiting to see the demonstration of mediumship. We entered to a chatter of excitement and I felt distracted by my thoughts. We took our seats and listened to the introductions, and then it was my turn to demonstrate. Since I began as a medium over twenty years ago, I always prepared in the same way: I focussed on my breath, my thoughts quietened and I moved my awareness to the Spirit

World, then I stood up to work. To my surprise, it was like every other demonstration I'd ever done. There was no change in the evidence, the content, my feelings or the recipients' responses; in all ways it was exactly the same as every other demonstration. After my allotted thirty minutes had passed, I sat down and reflected on the contrast between my thoughts before the demonstration and the subsequent experience of it. Putting aside my own thoughts and feelings, I realised that the experience of mediumship can only be affected by the energy of the environment in the *present* moment. Of course, the history of the gaol had been retained in its atmosphere, but as a medium, the difficult history of the building wasn't the source of my information. The source of information was from the loved ones who were connecting, and thankfully, I'd been able to move beyond my own thoughts, fears, beliefs and worry about the success of the demonstration such that I was able to hear them.

I've had the privilege of demonstrating mediumship in many venues around the world, ranging from spiritualist churches, theatres, pubs, prisons, hotels and church halls. The truth is that it isn't the physical environment that affects the quality of the demonstration. What the environment *can* do, however, is to influence the type of evidence that I receive from the Spirit World and also the recipient's response. For example, in venues where in order to book a ticket people have had to supply their full names and addresses, the evidence that comes forward from the Spirit World doesn't usually contain the recipient's names and addresses. Instead, the evidence is more about the loved one's experiences in life; it is full of their memories, and if there are names and other such information given, it's usually related to the communicator rather than to the recipients. Of course, the Spirit World want us to know it's real, and so they know they also need to change the evidence according to the environment and circumstances. The more specific the evidence we give as mediums, the more the sceptics will accuse us of 'hot' reading, meaning they think we've researched recipients prior to the demonstration. In response to this, I believe the Other World alters the type of evidence that is presented to us so that the reality of their presence still shines through. Once we trust our awareness, we are not alarmed when things change – they should change; mediumship is incredibly responsive to the inner and outer elements, and we must allow this happen.

Environment also influences the attitude and behaviour of the audience. Generally speaking, when demonstrating within a spiritualist church, the audiences aren't rowdy and they don't 'heckle', something which can occur in a public house or even a theatre! Receiving evidence of your loved one's survival is an incredibly intimate experience, some of which can be lost when demonstrating in an environment with a large audience. When we're demonstrating in public, of course we're there to give communication to the recipients, but we're also demonstrating the reality of the Spirit World to everyone else. It was the US psychologist Jonathan M. Freedman who, in his 1952 'density-intensity hypothesis', proposed that the bigger the audience, the more likely they are to act as one. He went on to suggest that audience reactions can be unpleasant in an unpleasant situation; conversely, they can be pleasant in a pleasant situation. It's therefore vital that we are able to 'hold' the audience's attention and ensure they are fully engaged and feeling positive.

There are certain forms of mediumship, the demonstration of which requires that the environment is strictly arranged, otherwise the phenomena of the Spirit World cannot occur, and this kind of mediumship can also be harmful to the medium if it is not properly monitored. For certain types of physical mediumship, the room must be completely blacked out and thoroughly cleaned, in order that no harm comes to the medium. There are stories of physical mediums sustaining burns from lights being switched on during interrupted séances. Even an instance where the room was not sufficiently cleaned prior to the séance, when metal pins remained on the floor – a medium was impaled by the pins as ectoplasm was withdrawn back into the medium. This form of physical mediumship is incredibly rare and the conditions for its demonstration have to be strictly controlled by the mediums and their circle leaders.

We must also consider whether the environment 'out there' can have an influence on the medium and mediumship. I have met many mediums over the years who claim that their awareness is affected and influenced by moon phases, thunder and lightning, sunshine, the seasons or any other external factors. It would be true to say that anything that affects our emotional state has the potential to affect our mediumship. Obviously, if you have a fear of thunder then you're going to find it more challenging to demonstrate in thundery conditions because you'd most likely rather be hiding under a table! The waxing and waning of the moon and its corresponding energy levels is often cited as the reason why some mediums prefer not to demonstrate at particular times of the month. I've greatly researched this in an attempt to find some scientific evidence relating to moon cycles and associated behaviour, mood changes and its effect on the emotions, but nothing definitive has come to light. I think it's true, therefore, to say that *anything* involving belief has the potential to become your experience. I think it's also fair to say that if we hold any particular opinion about how the environment can affect us, then we give power to that environment until it manifests as our experience. Since Belfast, I know from my own experience that, regardless of the environment or conditions I'm working in, if we allow it to, the power will move us beyond any fear, doubt or perceived limitations our thinking has created.

CHAPTER 16

LANGUAGE

"For the mouth speaks what the heart is full of."

Luke 6:45

We can all accept that words are powerful. The second they leave our minds they have a power in the world where hearts, minds and lives can be both built and broken by them. It matters not whether they are spoken or written; once we trace them back, they give us an insight into the mind and heart of the person who offered them to the world.

In an ideal world, we would all choose our words carefully. We would be mindful of their effect on others, and then modify any that we perceive could be hurtful or unkind without dishonouring ourselves or our truth. It's not just the words themselves which hold the power, it's also how we convey our feelings and thoughts – it's also the volume of them, the softness in our voice as we speak, the font we use when we write, and whether it's CAPITILISED, **in bold type**, *in italics*, underlined, or EVEN ALL OF THEM!

When we *know* the people we're speaking to are suffering, in need and in pain, we instinctively speak to them in a way which is kinder and softer. We know that one wrong word can be damaging, sometimes forever, and so we choose our words carefully. As mediums, we are generally *only* seeing people who are suffering; people don't come to us when all is well. When we don't choose the correct words, it's usually because we have identified more with our own thoughts and feelings, and have lost awareness of the effect our words might have on the receiver of them. When we can move out of our own 'stuff' and identify with someone else's reality, then our words have the potential to heal rather than harm. When we also add into that dynamic our connection to the greater power of love, and both our language and our presence is imbued with that power too, then healing is more available to them.

As we can see above, the language we use is influenced by the presence (or absence!) of our own mind, our connectedness to the power and also by the people we're communicating with. We must realise that not only can we influence a person through our words and our presence, but that this also contributes to the environment we're working in. The energy of our words hangs in the air around us and has the potential to influence the experience of mediumship, as well as what recipients and observers offer of themselves to the process.

Another way in which our words can influence our experience is in our direct interactions with the Spirit World.

I've noticed over the years working as an evidential medium and as a teacher, that our awareness of the Spirit World and the language we use is directly connected. The connector of the two shows where our consciousness is in the process. When you watch a medium demonstrate, you will often hear them use phrases such as 'I feel…', 'I see…' and 'I know…', but less often, 'I think…' This suggests that in the receipt of information from the Spirit World that it's coming through our awareness and feeling state rather than our own thinking. This is absolutely true, although what it *doesn't* suggest is the origin of that information. Are they aware of the information coming from somewhere in the room by reading the memory of the environment, is it from a person who is present (both psychic connections) or is it actually coming from a person who is communicating from the Other Side?

I classify mediumistic awareness into two distinct categories: *perception* and *presence*. Perception suggests that something is separate to you; there is some degree of 'space' between you and 'it', but yet you still have an awareness of it. In the 'space' between you and it, there is room for you to make assumptions, assessments, judgements and have opinions on the thing you're aware of – in effect, there's room for your mind to be present. Some of those perceptions may be accurate, but undoubtedly some of those will be incorrect as the mind makes up a story about its observations.

As we move more into the presence of the communicator, our perceptions of them as being separate to us subside and our minds become less involved, but our awareness of them deepens. We then get to know who they are through the experience of our awareness rather than through the opinions of our mind. The language we use when working from the perspective of presence is vastly different. Instead of the 'I'm aware of...' language when we're perceiving them, it becomes much clearer and more statement-orientated. We'll find ourselves saying 'He is...', 'She says...' and 'There is...', which not only demonstrates the reality of our awareness and connection in that moment, but to the observer it also displays the origin of the information too.

We can look to remove the word 'I' from mediumship consciously, but this conscious involvement of the mind will continue to involve you in the process. Instead, work towards developing a closer relationship to the Spirit World, and in doing so your mind will become less involved. When this happens, the language you use will automatically change.

Another thing that occurs when we're working only from perception is that we can have an awareness of what we're NOT receiving. We'll say things like, "I'm not getting his name..." or, "I don't know what that means," which, quite honestly, is really not helpful to anyone. When we're speaking about what we're *not* receiving, we're actually affirming the absence of the presence in our mediumship.

This negative affirmation isn't just limited to the evidence the mediums are open to either; sometimes it's also related to their experience of the Spirit World as whole. They may talk about which of their senses 'work' and which don't – either they see or don't, hear or don't, etc. In truth, all this suggests is that they're not allowing enough of themselves to be utilised by the Other World, because every type of evidence and mediumistic sense *is* available to us in our mediumship, but the language we use contributes to shaping the experience.

The last point I want to make in relation to language is this: what words do you use to define yourself? Whether these are spoken or not, written down or not, what is the inner dialogue you attach to you, your awareness, your mediumship and your role? Even your name has a power attached to it – have you ever researched the meaning of it? When we take ourselves into the power, what is returned through the experience of our mediumship will both reflect us *and* the Spirit communicator. In our attempts to be the best mediums for the Spirit World as possible, I refer to my nanna's advice from when I was very young: "Watch your language." I know she meant it in a very different way back then, but it really is an indicator of what's happening on the inside, and in mediumship it's wise to recognise its importance.

CHAPTER 17

EXPRESSION

"You're going to have two children in your life. The first one will be a boy, and he'll be healthy and strong. The second one will be a girl, and she'll be born deformed."

"There's a death coming in your close family – I see the initial 'E.'"

"You're gay, aren't you?"

"You were abused in a past life and you've brought that in with you when you were born, so you're going to be abused in this one."

"Because your son killed himself, he doesn't go to the same place in the Spirit World with everyone else in your family."

"Did your grandad pee himself before he died? I see an old man here wearing a hospital gown with a big yellow stain on it."

How does it feel to read those statements? How might it feel to hear if you were pregnant with your second child, nursing a sick loved one, gay and ashamed, were in grief, were fearful for your future, or your grandad had passed away and you believed he was being cared for well in hospital? Can you just imagine the awful feelings those statements might evoke within you and even more so if said in a public arena, having heard other communications that were evidential and accurate?

Sadly, the above statements are some examples of things I have heard, witnessed and also directly experienced made by so-called mediums to me and to others. To understand why these statements are made and where they come from, we must look at our beliefs about the Spirit World and also how we view it.

Over many years I have met those mediums who hold the attitude 'I just give what I get and Spirit are always right', regardless of the pain or anxiety it may cause, and I have also met those who are frightened to cause any harm or anxiety, to the extent that they say nothing at all. So, is there a right way to deliver a communication from the Spirit World?

Absolutely, first and foremost, 'Do no harm', which in any language, culture, religion or belief system is sound advice, although the different definitions of 'harm' may encourage some people to speak nonsense because of their version of what is, or is not, harmful. Let me be clear: as a human being sharing the planet with others and hopefully making it a better place, we should not in ANY capacity be unkind, or unloving, or belittle people with our words, thoughts or deeds; we need to be very conscious of what we say at ALL times.

Within the spiritual arena, people have an expectation that we are kind, thoughtful and compassionate. We also have to be aware that the people we see in our work may be vulnerable themselves. We have a responsibility to be authentic and aware of the power and impact that our words can have, especially when they could have a life-changing effect.

I can fully understand that sometimes we just accept and repeat what we've been told by our teachers. We absorb their views and 'framework' of how the experience of mediumship should be, so our awareness will actually conform to that, however dysfunctional or damaging it is.

I remember being told that when we see the colour blue, it means healing energy, and I believed this for years, even though my experience of the colour was very different. I tried to make my own awareness fit that definition because I trusted in my teachers, their experience and authority – in effect, I became a copy of their experience and had not developed my own views. A good teacher should help you recognise how *your* unique awareness functions specifically for you. Likewise, if a teacher creates fear within the student by being discouraging, unkind, unloving or aggressive, then I urge you to find another teacher, because you will not flourish under these conditions and actually may inadvertently absorb it and become that yourself. Don't be afraid to question what you are being taught if it feels inauthentic to you.

The second part of this question is really about your perception of the Spirit World or God. Do you believe that God is punitive, that there is a right or wrong way to live, and that the Spirit World knows everything about everyone and they are never wrong? As a medium, do you believe that you're so infallible that everything you say is from the

Spirit World and there's no room for error in what you communicate? Or do you simply not know enough about how your awareness and mediumship works, that you're ignorant of the responsibility it entails? If you answer yes to any of these questions (and it takes guts to be honest with ourselves), then you may as well be driving a truck with poor eyesight and no licence!

If you are serious about this work, if you care about people and you want to help to 'elevate' them in some way, it is vital that we ask ourselves these questions regularly and check in with what our motivation really is for doing this work.

So, I want you to imagine that we are like three layers of an onion. Those 'layers' working from outside to inside are physical body, Spirit and soul. The physical body is the obvious part in this, but it's the other elements that are the more significant aspects.

I acknowledge that at the core of who I am, in my SOUL, I hold within me qualities of love, kindness, healing, empathy and wisdom. I also recognise that in my SPIRIT, which co-exists with my soul, I am also able to have and hold my own opinions, beliefs, fears and judgements about people and about life. These two aspects of the self operate together, often interchangeably, and there are times when I'm more in touch with one than the other.

When I'm operating from my soul's perspective, I am kinder, more loving, less judgemental and more accepting of others. When I operate exclusively from my Spirit, I am more opinionated, need to be right, feel fearful, am not as kind or as loving as is possible, and I'm also aware of this.

Mediumship and intuitive work is soul work, meaning that when we are operating from this 'place', we embody the soul's qualities and are also in touch with a desire to elevate others. The word desire actually comes from Latin and has a sacred meaning: 'De Sire', meaning 'Of the Father', suggesting that whatever becomes manifest through desire must also show up in a divine or godly way.

When demonstrating mediumship, whether in public or private, we are not only demonstrating the reality of a loved one's survival of 'death', but we are also demonstrating the reality of the soul and the Spirit within us. We reveal ourselves through our work, and so our delivery of information and its origin is reflected in our words and in our behaviours. If, in the name of this work and through your words or actions, you are creating within another person anxiety or fear, AND/OR you are giving to yourself a feeling of being in some way 'more' because of it, you are not operating fully from your soul. If we witness that kind of mediumship, and inevitably we will, then we should question it and not tolerate it. Do not accept communications from mediums or psychics who predict death, misery, illness or any other kind of advice that moves you into fear. Of course, I cannot compel you to take this advice, as you have free will. But if you chose to listen to negative predictions, and I will make my own prediction for you here, you will be unable to live your life fully in the moment and be happy – one eye will forever be on the future, looking out for some tragedy to befall you or your family so you can prove the harbinger of doom was right!

So how do we ensure that we're operating from the soul's perspective when we work? Simply remember how it began.

Before I begin to work, I take a few moments to think back to the time when I was first touched by the reality of the Spirit World, and I relive and recapture the positive emotions it evoked within me; I then embrace those feelings in that moment. Everyone's experience will be different. It may be that you dreamed of a loved one and woke up just knowing you had been with them. It could be the time you heard your name called and then forever wondered, "Was that them?" It could be that you got an amazing communication through a medium which left you in no doubt of their presence. Whatever took you to that emotional place of acceptance, reunion and love – use that.

For myself, I remember my wonder at knowing that the Spirit World was real, and I bring that feeling of it into the now. I can't help but feel joy knowing there is no death, and how in this moment I can't ever dishonour what I now know. I accept the feeling that my life and its meaning was transformed from that moment onwards. I now know that I will see my loved ones again, and I know that because they survived death, then so will I. The knowledge of this fills my heart and I want to share this new-found awareness and reality with others.

The Spirit World is right beside me always, closer than breath, and is only ever separated from me when I hold the belief that they're not. I know they're here and they want others to know it too. In essence, I 'lean in to' my soul and, using those feelings, I allow it to 'hold me' and therefore be the author of the experience. In doing so, not only is the presence of my own soul apparent by the expression of the qualities it holds, but also the content and delivery of the communication with the Spirit World becomes more tangible. This experience also has the potential of providing a therapeutic benefit to the recipients and observers by their participation.

CHAPTER 18

FINAL THOUGHTS

Mediumistic development is an ongoing process; there is never a place where we've finished unfolding our awareness or uncovering different parts of ourselves. In this book I've attempted to offer you, the unfolding medium, my thoughts and my experiences in a way which may help you to find your unique style and your own relationship with those in the Spirit World. In offering this to you, I also want to remind you that you will never retire from being a medium. Whether you actively demonstrate mediumship or not, whether you teach it privately or publicly or not, whether you walk away from it or not, you will never stop being a medium.

The blessing of mediumship is that it reminds us that we already ARE Spirit and as such, when we move on to the Other World, we continue to be *and* evolve to be more. Mediumship, on this level, offers us the opportunity to have that reunion with our loved ones before we get to the Spirit World ourselves. When we know from our experience that is true, we can never forget it, and so we are forever a conduit between the tangible and the intangible. Beyond all of that, we also know that our very presence in the world is also a demonstration of our soul's need to evolve and to assist others in doing so too. Who we are is limitless, in presence and potential, and spiritual unfoldment of any kind is really just about remembering this. You can't ever *un*-know this.

To assist you in remembering this, and to expand your ongoing unfoldment, following these activities may help:

- Examine self through personal development, i.e. therapy, journaling, etc.
- Take time to sit and blend with Spirit regularly and be led by them.
- Experience is the greatest teacher – be open to it, however it feels.

"Your task is not to seek love, but merely to find all the barriers within yourself that you have built against it."

Rumi